HIDDEN HISTORY *in the*
WELSH MOUNTAINS

Richard Hayman

LOGASTON PRESS

FRONT COVER: A ruined farm building in the hills above Dyffryn Ardudwy.
BACK COVER: A late-Victorian milestone on the road between Capel Curig and Beddgelert.
FRONTISPIECE: A remote hillside on the west side of Yr Wyddfa.

First published November 2024 by Logaston Press
The Holme, Church Road, Eardisley HR3 6NJ
www.logastonpress.co.uk
An imprint of Fircone Books Ltd.

ISBN 978-1-910839-80-5

Designed by Richard Wheeler in 11 on 15 Garamond.
Cover design by Richard Wheeler.

Printed and bound in Poland www.lfbookservices.co.uk

Logaston Press is committed to a sustainable future for our business, our readers and our planet.
The book in your hands is made of FSC® certified and other controlled material.

MIX
Paper | Supporting
responsible forestry
FSC® C105618
FSC
www.fsc.org

British Library Catalogue in Publishing Data.
A CIP catalogue record for this book is available from the British Library.

CONTENTS

ACKNOWLEDGEMENTS

This book was born out of domestic confinement – a determination to revisit the Welsh mountains that grew during the months in 2020 and 2021 when lockdowns and other restrictions prevented or significantly limited access to the great outdoors. Many of the places described in this book were already familiar to me. Between 2000 and 2014 I was lucky enough to walk the hills of Wales surveying its archaeology, contributing to the uplands initiative organised by the Royal Commission on the Ancient and Historical Monuments of Wales (RCAHM Wales). I did not do this alone, and other people have contributed indirectly to this book. The surveys were done in partnership with Wendy Horton and were managed by David Leighton of RCAHM Wales, while much was learned in annual forums reporting on the uplands initiative.

The basic skills needed to recognise archaeological features in the landscape can be acquired through practice and a little curiosity. To help you, there are a variety of resources that can guide you to finding out more.

One of the basic skills is the ability to read a map, and we are lucky to have the detailed maps produced by the Ordnance Survey that really enrich our experience of the great outdoors. For mountain landscapes, the most suitable maps are the Ordnance Survey Explorer series, at a scale of 1:25,000. They can be used in digital form when downloaded to tablets and smart phones, or used in hard-copy format. For the latter there is a sub-series known as Outdoor Leisure maps that cover the National Parks of Eryri, Bannau Brycheiniog and the Pembrokeshire Coast, which includes the Preseli Hills. Explorer maps have an impressive level of detail, including many historic and archaeological features, which are identified by the use of italics. They also clearly mark rights of way and areas of access land in upland landscapes. Points on the map are located by grid references, which are expressed as the horizontal (or easting) coordinate, followed by the vertical (or northing). The Ordnance Survey grid is composed of kilometre squares. To make it easier to use, it is divided into 100 kilometre squares with a letter prefix. So, for example, the Roman fort at Tomen y Mur in Eryri is at SH 7060 3865, which gives an accuracy to the nearest 10 metres. The letter prefix denotes the 100 kilometre square, then there are the four-figure eastings and northings (making up an eight-figure grid reference).

Ordnance Survey grid references can be established in the field by using a GPS device. This is particularly useful if you come across a feature that is not marked on the OS map. In practice it is not necessary to purchase a GPS receiver – which gives a reading for up to 4 metres accuracy – as there are many free apps for smart phones that will give an accuracy to 10 metres, or an 8-figure grid reference. There are online resources that can help to identify these features once you get home, or which can be consulted before heading out on to the hills, to give you an idea of what to expect. These use grid references, which is the main reason for recommending them. Co-ordinates expressed as latitude and longitude are increasingly popular with outdoor enthusiasts but archaeological features are not recorded in this format and it is not possible to apply these co-ordinates to Ordnance Survey maps. For that reason they are not recommended for identifying archaeological features. The same flaw applies to the 'what3words' application. I have often noted down grid references of interesting features on a map and then used a phone or GPS to help me navigate to the right spot.

Information on archaeological sites is held on publicly-accessible databases. There are four regional Historic Environment Records (HER) databases covering Wales, which can all be consulted at www.archwilio.org.uk. There is also a National Monuments Record maintained by the Royal Commission on the Ancient and Historical Monuments of Wales (RCAHM Wales for short), which can be found at www.coflein.gov.uk. These entries vary from brief sentences that simply record the existence of a feature, to some longer entries with photographs and, if you are lucky, a link to a more detailed study.

The more important archaeological and historical sites are protected by government legislation. Scheduled Monuments are protected archaeological sites which, although many of them have features above ground like standing stones and industrial buildings, are likely to retain important archaeological evidence below ground. Listed Buildings occur much less frequently in upland landscapes, for obvious reasons, but there are nevertheless examples such as houses and milestones. The responsible body for designating heritage assets is Cadw, which maintains a website at www.cadw.gov.wales/advice-support/cof-cymru. The site allows searches by map. A separate website covering all of the information held by Cadw, the regional Historic Environment Records and the National Monuments Record is at www.historicwales.gov.uk. It is fair to say that the Scheduled and Listed sites will be among the 'best' upland sites to visit. These designated monuments are tilted in favour of older and rarer sites, like cairns, since rarity makes a pressing case for preservation, leaving out many of the more common post-medieval features, although this imbalance is slowly changing. The extent and diversity of archaeological sites from the post-medieval centuries has only been appreciated more recently as the archaeological profession has developed and acquired its expertise in those areas.

Historic Landscape Characterisation has been undertaken across many parts of Wales, including the unenclosed uplands. There is a register of landscapes of outstanding historic interest, some of which are accessible on the websites of the component parts of Heneb: The Trust for Archaeology in Wales. The website www.dyfedarchaeology.org.uk/HLC//HistoricLandscapeCharacterisation.htm covers south-west Wales, including the Preseli Hills and part of the Bannau Brycheiniog National Park. The Eryri landscape is covered at www.heneb.co.uk/hlc/hlc.html. The landscapes of north-east Wales, including the Berwyn Mountains and Mynydd Hiraethog, and into the Bannau Brycheiniog National Park, can be found at www.cpat.org.uk/projects/longer/histland/histland.htm. These individual studies look closely at the processes that have shaped the landscape, and are a good source of background information. A list of historic place-names in Wales has also been curated at www.historicplacenames.rcahmw.gov.uk/.

Other useful sources of information are historic maps, satellite imagery and LiDAR imagery. A variety of historic maps are available online. Tithe maps were drawn up by parishes in Wales in the 1830s and 1840s and, although moorland is often left blank, some have useful information on the extent of sheepwalks or of farmsteads that have since been abandoned. They are available to view from the National Library of Wales at www.places.library.wales/. The Ordnance Survey has been mapping Wales since the early nineteenth century. The original survey drawings for the 1-inch maps are held at the British Library and can be viewed online. The most useful of the maps are the county-series maps, compiled between the 1870s and the 1940s, which run in most parts to three or four editions, with important revisions. The maps were drawn at two scales: 1:2,500, or roughly 25 inches to the mile, and 1:10,560, or 6 inches to the mile. The first edition of the latter can be found as one of the overlays on the tithe maps resource mentioned above. The best resource can be found at www.maps.nls.uk/. Unfortunately, for upland landscapes it contains few of the 25-inch surveys but it does have the smaller 6-inch maps, which include almost as much detail.

Satellite imagery has become widely used in recent decades and some resources are available online. A useful source that allows you to view satellite imagery over modern Ordnance Survey mapping is www.bing.com/maps. The disadvantage of satellite imagery, however, is that the images are taken from a vertical angle and the results are often quite flat, making it difficult to distinguish features of interest.

LiDAR (which stands for Light Detection and Ranging) is an airborne mapping technique using lasers to provide accurate measurements of the height of terrain, producing imagery that, in black and white, looks like a photograph but in fact contains more accurate information and is able to see through tree canopies. Not all of the uplands have been covered using this technique, but there are some areas where it can be used profitably and it is fun to try out. LiDAR data is available online in map form at www.datamap.gov.wales/maps/lidar-viewer/view#/.

Aerial photography has been an important tool for archaeologists since the 1920s and there is a vast archive of aerial images available online. Some of the images taken by RCAHM Wales are available on its Coflein website. Aerofilms was a private company that undertook aerial surveys from 1919 to 2006, the archive of which is known as Britain from Above and is available online at www.britainfroma-bove.org.uk/ (a Welsh language version is also available). However, the uplands are only sparsely covered in this archive.

Guides to specific types of archaeological sites are included in the reading list. There are also online sites that cover a surprising range of features and are usually well-informed. Sites such as www.megalithic. co.uk and www.themodernantiquarian.com are a fund of useful information. A project to photograph every square kilometre in Britain is at www.geograph.org.uk/ which is an open online community where pictures of all sorts of historic features can be shared, along with general landscape photographs. That said, they cover mostly the ancient and/or well-known sites. But there are thousands more modest features that may be unremarkable but contribute to a fascinating story of everyday lives in the landscape, for which there is no real guide and for which this book has been written.

Living in the presence of mountains, like here in the quarry village of Nantlle (Gwynedd), has ensured that the mountains have been at the heart of Wales and Welshness.

1

Mynydd and the nature of uplands in Wales

I T is common to hear Welsh people speak of mountains, even though, by European standards, nothing rises to any great height in Wales. The official definition of a mountain in Britain is a landform that rises to over 600m (1,969 feet) above sea level, of which there are eight in Wales. But that is not really the point. In the English language the word *mountain* conjures images of snow-capped peaks, a place to conquer the summit and come back down again, somewhere remote and ordinarily inaccessible. But when it is applied to Wales it is used as the nearest equivalent to the word *mynydd*. In Wales the mountains are rarely snow-capped and have never been either remote or inaccessible. Look at any large scale Ordnance Survey map of high ground in Wales and you will see that it is littered with names for crags and streams. Every named *cwm*, *coed*, *graig*, *ffynnon* or *waun* is evidence of a place whose character has been intimately known and understood. It is the world of these people, to whom the mountains – or *mynydd* – were a familiar part of everyday life, that this books sets out to recover.

The hills of Wales are now a place of escape for people living in more populous parts of the country, or working in stressful human environments. See another human being on the hills and they are most likely to be hiking or biking, and very unlikely to be making a living from the land. The implications of this are brought home as soon as you encounter the bottlenecks around the summit routes to Yr Wyddfa (Snowdon). Begin at the busy Rhyd Ddu car park, for example, you invariably join a long procession of walkers, but almost all of them will be intent on conquering the summit. Step off the main track, head up to the old Cwm y Llan slate quarry, and an empty Eryri (Snowdonia) awaits. There is nobody there.

The modern mindset sees a mountain as an occasional place where the ground is traversed in a route to the summit. But in the past people inhabited the mountain in a different way, when long familiarity taught farmers, shepherds, miners and quarrymen to avoid the boggy ground and the windy spots, giving them the skills to traverse difficult terrain with apparent ease. George Borrow recognised this when he walked on Plynlimon with a local shepherd in the mid-nineteenth century:

> My guide walked with a calm and deliberate gait, yet I had considerable difficulty in keeping up with him. ... he was a shepherd walking on his own hill, and having first-rate wind, and knowing every inch of the ground, made great way without seeming to be in the slightest hurry.

Mynydd in Wales is the land above the normal grazing in fields, usually in recent centuries left to sheep and goats, sometimes encompassing places where peat could be cut, as we will see later. In that sense, the *mynydd* has been an integral part of the Welsh economy for centuries. It continues to be so, but in a different way now that the landscape has become a cultural resource drawing many visitors from across the border.

Archaeologists who study these landscapes have been familiar with the distinction between the Highland and Lowland Zones, essentially a distinction between two forms of land use, that were first defined in the mid-twentieth century by Sir Cyril Fox, Director of the National Museum of Wales. However, defining what is and what is not highland, *mynydd* or uplands, is not a precise science. Since 2000 there has been a right to roam on most of the high ground in Wales, which can be identified by the shading on the larger-scale Ordnance Survey maps. This access land could be one definition, albeit not a perfect one. In practice not all of it is open moorland, as it includes land that was enclosed by field walls that are now defunct, while there is some open moorland that has not been designated as access land. For that reason *moorland* will not quite work as a definition either. It could be land above a certain contour, but in practice again the character of moorland can be found at different altitudes. So whereas there is moorland at 200m above sea level in South Wales there is also plenty of land at that altitude that remains as fields of improved grass bound by fences or drystone walls. The concept of common land as we understand it in the modern world does not help much either. It is English in origin, and has been applied to Wales only since the Act of Union of 1536. In reality common land applies to only a small proportion of high ground in Wales, or any type of ground for that matter, and is most prevalent in the border counties. So we have to accept that what constitutes mountain land or uplands cannot be tied to a precise definition, but is perhaps best defined as a character of landscape. You know it when you see it.

Cefn-hir Uchaf near Llynnau Cregennen (Gwynedd) is a farmstead that, typically, marks the meeting of lowland and upland landscapes.

The uplands through time

Most of us who visit the mountains of Wales are looking for its wildness, so we usually pay little heed to the landscape's human traces. These places are no longer part of a domestic and familiar world. But the mountainous regions of Wales are to a large extent a by-product of human history. There is certainly wildness in these places, but any notion that they are a pure manifestation of nature is illusory. In Wales (as in the remainder of Britain) there is not really any such thing as a wilderness – a place untouched by human society. The idea that these upland landscapes have always been remote and uninhabited places exists only inside our heads. If it is now a wilderness, it is not because it has never been inhabited, but because it has been abandoned.

The archaeology of the uplands of Wales has a historic depth and diversity, and is an important part of the nation's cultural history. It is worth remembering that such places are only viewed as outlying or remote to those viewing them from an urban perspective. Mountains may be places that we like to escape to, but in the past – for the slate workers of Eryri or the metal miners of the Cambrian Mountains – living the week in barracks, the mountains might have been a place to escape *from*.

The outline story of how mountains and moorlands have been used in history is well known, so what follows is only a brief sketch. The story of uplands as uplands really begins with the retreat of the ice at the end of the last Ice Age.

Maen Serth, near Rhayader (Powys), has many layers of history – maybe a prehistoric standing stone, with a cross incised on it in medieval times, standing beside an old route across the Cambrian Mountains, perhaps used by pilgrims.

The ice once covered all of the land mass of Wales and its retreat created the topography we are now familiar with. Neanderthals and modern humans had walked over these hills before, but the action of the ice sheets scraped away any surface evidence they may have left behind, with the exception of the archaeology found in caves, which were protected

A remote-looking hillside on the west side of Yr Wyddfa (Gwynedd) may at first glance appear to be a wilderness, but look closely and there are field walls and a ruined farm building.

from the relentless grind of the ice. There has been a persistent belief that, left to its own devices, the landscapes of Britain were a continuous forest until they were progressively cleared for farming. But the higher ground could never have been carpeted over with trees. The ground is too stony, in many places had only very thin soils and was often poorly drained at that. So a world of scattered trees, grass and exposed rocks is the kind of landscape settlers found when they reached the high ground of Wales at the end of the last Ice Age.

Post-glacial hunter-gatherers (or Mesolithic people) returned to Wales about 14,500 years ago, but if they inhabited the uplands they trod very lightly here. It is a period that leaves little traces, principally collections of artefacts. That said, there have been comparatively few excavations of prehistoric sites on the uplands, and few potential settlements have ever been identified. These are usually caves used as shelters, a good example of which is the re-occupation of Paviland cave on the Gower about 12,500 years ago. At this time the sea level was lower

Maengwyngweddw, above the Elan Valley in Powys, is a quartz boulder beside a track that might once have been part of the Aberystwyth Mountain Road, the medieval Monk's Trod, or both. It may be prehistoric, it may be a former boundary stone. What is more certain is that it is one of the loose stones that littered the natural landscape of Wales.

Loose surface stones have been put to good use in Wales. Upland buildings, like this farm building in the hills above Dyffryn Ardudwy (Gwynedd), have very often been built with the stones that once littered the landscape.

and so the Gower looked out over the lower Severn Valley, not the sea as it does today. (The famous Red Lady of Paviland – actually a man – was a pre-glacial burial carried out 26,000 years ago.)

It was the Neolithic communities that first started altering the earth with their monument construction. Neolithic (c.4000BC to 2300BC) is distinguished from the earlier Mesolithic as it includes arte-facts associated with settled farming. The term Neolithic may be in common use but is not especially helpful for our purposes, especially as it has long been noted that some of the earliest monumental construc-tions appeared on the Atlantic fringes of Europe where the Mesolithic persisted the longest. The permanent legacy of this period is, if not the first, then at least the earliest-surviving; evidence of people deliberately writing history into the landscape. There may once have been earlier rock art created by hunter-gatherers, but subsequent ice sheets have ensured that if any existed across the landscapes of Wales, they were scraped away by the debris under moving ice.

Standing stones like this upright boulder above Penmaenmawr in Eryri are one of the oldest examples of deliberately writing history into the landscape.

Ty Newydd standing stones in the Preseli Hills (Pembrokeshire) are probably naturally-occurring slabs raised upright.

Three hilltop cairns on Foel Drygarn in the Preseli Hills (Pembrokeshire) were later enclosed within an Iron Age hillfort.

The conventional wisdom that the Neolithic brought farming techniques, and therefore a settled lifestyle in contrast to the earlier hunter-gatherer lifestyle, is long outdated. There is very little evidence of permanent settlement in Neolithic Wales, possibly because there was very little permanent settlement. In any case, direct evidence of farming in the Neolithic is not found in the uplands. The absence of domestic evidence in comparison with funeral monuments suggests a more mobile population, perhaps crossing the relatively open higher ground on a seasonal basis. The creation of ritual landscapes and the grouping of funeral monuments to create cairn cemeteries does suggest a territorial factor in their construction, and the attachment of communities to specific places.

From the Middle Bronze Age onwards (from *c*.1200BC) everything starts to change. The later Bronze Age and the Iron Age (from *c*.800BC) are characterised by the archaeology of secular life, be it the multitude of former roundhouses that can be identified on the hills to the more famous hillforts, a precise and universal interpretation of which has been elusive. The period of Roman occupation is largely one of continuity in the Welsh hills. The Roman imprint is seen in its military fortifications and the road network that served them. Gradually the form of settlements changed into the medieval period, where houses now adopted a rectangular plan and farmsteads were created on the large monastic estates.

There was upland industry in medieval Wales, but it only started to have a major impact on the landscape from the end of the eighteenth century. Upland industry means exploitation of raw materials, and the geology of Wales has been a rich resource that has made fortunes for some people, has induced folly in less-savvy entrepreneurs and pulled many people across and into Wales. Coal and iron mining turned the upland landscapes on the fringe of the Bannau Brycheiniog National Park into a world leader in iron and steel manufacture; slate quarrying and mining transformed landscapes and society, especially in Eryri; but there have also been metal mines, for lead, copper, silver and gold, in the ancient hard rocks of the more thinly-populated Cambrian Mountains.

The industrial revolution also spawned the steam railway, which had a transformative power over rural and upland landscapes unlike anything that had been seen before. Railways reached the more sparsely peopled parts of Wales, giving them connections to a much wider world. There have been several important consequences. The benefits to the upland regions of Wales have been, at best, mixed, as the new transport infrastructure created a society and economy that could be controlled from the centre. Upland farming declined as people found it easy to leave to find work in the large industrial concerns, be it the coal and iron industries of South Wales or slate quarrying in the north. Later on, land of little value was ripe for infrastructure projects such

The shifting nature of landscape – Blaenau Ffestiniog is an industrial town built on what would otherwise be regarded as an upland landscape.

There has been industry on the mountains of Wales since prehistory, but little of the evidence you will see is earlier than the nineteenth century. Bryn Glas Quarry near Llan Ffestiniog was worked from the 1890s to the 1920s.

The line of an industrial railway at the Bwlch Camllan slate quarry in Eryri.

Abandoned farmsteads are a common sight in the Welsh hills, a consequence of changing farming practices and our increasingly urbanised society.

as forestry, reservoirs and wind farms, all of which have made a significant impact on the landscape and all of which have been resented to varying degrees. They certainly changed the culture of upland life. The day-to-day management of the mountain regions has increasingly been decided in faraway cities like London and Cardiff. This includes not only the Acts of Parliament necessary for the creation of reservoirs, but the designation of National Parks and Areas of Outstanding Natural Beauty. In many of the popular mountain districts the majority of the population is now made up of visitors, and tourism has long overtaken agriculture and industry as the mainstay of local economies.

One of the first ways that the upland economy was diversified was by forestry. The Forestry Commission was set up after the First World War to supply timber for industry; but it generally occurred on land that had previously been enclosed, as opposed to the open moorland. One of the arguments in favour of it was that it could offer employment to local people in remote areas where the farming economy had declined. However, the most contentious re-use of upland landscapes is the large-scale reservoirs that began, in Wales at least, with Lake Vyrnwy, and again offered a modicum of local employment. The use of the uplands for infrastructure has continued with the building of large wind farms from the late twentieth century onwards, which is not a significant local employer and adds to the general view that the uplands are not otherwise very economically productive, in a world where real estate is expected to earn its keep. It encourages the prevailing notion that the mountains are spare land outside the orbit of daily life and not essential to it. The people who think like that are unlikely to find much joy in this book.

THE LANGUAGE IN THE LANDSCAPE

The rich cultural history of the uplands of Wales is obvious simply by looking at an Ordnance Survey map. The Welsh language is written into the landscape of Wales and for many visitors, even long-term residents, this is a common stumbling block. Welsh is a notoriously difficult language for English-speaking adults to learn, but the least we can do is acknowledge its importance. There are a few basic rules that help. There is no 'v' in the Welsh alphabet. In Welsh the letter 'f' is equivalent to the English 'v', so the Welsh *fan* is pronounced 'van', while the equivalent of the English 'f' is 'ff', as in *fforest*. Other sounds do not have individual letters in the alphabet: 'll' is pronounced roughly 'thl' in English, while 'dd' is pronounced 'th', so that *Rhyd Ddu* is pronounced 'Reed thee'. The apparent lack of vowels also baffles non-Welsh speakers, but it helps to know that 'w' is pronounced 'oo', hence *Bwlch* is 'Boolk', and 'y' can be pronounced as a 'u' or 'i' in English, so *mynydd* is pronounced 'mun-ith'.

Welsh place-names are highly descriptive, deriving almost entirely from a single language (and as a consequence are more intelligible than the Anglo-Saxon, Norse and Norman French derivations found across the border). Just as the Inuit have many words for snow, Welsh has many names for hills and hillsides, including *allt, banc, bron/fron, bryn, clawdd, mynydd, rhiw*, with specific words for their crests or peaks (*cribyn, foel/moel, fan*), and ridges (*aran, cefn, esgair*). *Rhos* and *waun* are common upland place-names, meaning moorland, while there are words for heather (*grug*) and a variety of words for rocks and stones (*carn/garn, carreg/garreg, craig/graig, darren/tarren*). *Carreg* can refer to natural or standing stones, although *maen* is more common for artificially raised stones. *Carn* self-evidently refers to cairns, but it can also refer to natural rocky peaks.

Place-names in Wales also refer to human interaction with the hills, and can sometimes reveal the history of a place where there are no archaeological remains. The basic distinction in farming in Wales is between the *bro* – lowland – and the *blaenau* – the upland; or, more specifically, the head of a river valley. In Glamorgan, for example, the *bro* referred to the Vale lowlands and coastal belt, while the *blaenau* described the hills and steep-sided valleys to the north. Upland farming also has a distinction between the winter farmstead and the summer pasture, or the *hendre* and *hafod*. *Hafod* refers to the summer pasture rather than the house used during the summer, which is known as the *hafotty* (plural *hafotai*). Where the summer house was used as a dairy it is also known as a *lluest*, especially in mid Wales. Another word for upland pasture is the *ffridd* (plural *ffriddoedd*), which is enclosed land immediately below the open moorland. Areas of peat bog that were cut for fuel, usually known as 'turbaries', can be identified on maps by the *mawn* or *fawnog* element in place-names.

The Ordnance Survey has done a great service by preserving place-names on its maps; names that might otherwise have been forgotten, many of which are a part of local, not national, culture. The Ordnance Survey has also made some notable errors. It misinterpreted the first word of 'Erw Hepste', combining it with the local word *sgwd* for a waterfall, and hence renamed the famous waterfall in the Bannau Brycheiniog National Park as Sgwd yr Eira, 'the waterfall of snow', much more evocative than the original 'falls on the Hepste', but a modern name nonetheless. The recent decision by its National Park to drop the English names Snowdon and Snowdonia and to use only the Welsh names Yr Wyddfa and Eryri is a recognition of the importance of the language of place-names and provides an opportunity to promote the Welsh language and culture to a wider world. The Brecon Beacons National Park has followed suit by deciding to use only the Welsh name Bannau Brycheiniog from now on. Brecon Beacons is a relatively recent name, as is the Cambrian Mountains further north, which may one day return to their original name of Elenydd. Ironically Yr Wyddfa is the only mountain in Wales to have a separate English name. In his 1188 *Journey Through Wales* Gerald of Wales noted that the English knew Yr Wyddfa and Eryri as Snowdon and the Snow Mountains. It is marked as Snowdon on the map drawn *c.*1250 by Matthew Paris, a monk at St Albans Abbey. John Leland used only the Welsh terms when he described Caernarfonshire in the 1530s, although he also called Yr Wyddfa 'Craig Eryri'. Likewise William Camden described it as Craig Eryri in his *Britannia*, published in 1586, but also noted its English name. 'Snowdon' has become part of the mountain's cultural heritage as the place in Wales whose fame has spread most successfully beyond its borders.

Place-names are also the principal means by which the culture and history of Wales is represented in upland landscapes. Beddau Gwyr Ardudwy (SH 7230 4258), near Llan Ffestiniog, are not really the graves of the men of Ardudwy. Once it was a place where 30 low mounds could be seen, and they have perplexed antiquaries since Edward Lhuyd first mentioned them in the seventeenth century. Now there are only eight mounds left, reduced in size and quite difficult to pick out, but investigations have suggested they are nothing more than old peat stacks. It is not the bones of long-dead men that matter here, but the idea of them. History is not just about the things that happened, but about what people thought had happened. In Wales many of these stories are written into the landscape. Perhaps the most common associations in the Welsh mountains are with Arthurian legend. These are not necessarily very ancient. Arthurian place-names became fashionable in the Middle Ages in response to the popularity of Geoffrey of Monmouth's *History of the Kings of Britain*, written in the 1130s, and the appropriation of Arthur to the needs of the French-born English kings. Their appearance in Wales may have the same origin as those in England and

Scotland (and France). But some associations are earlier. Carn Gafallt, the steep mountain on the south side of the Elan Valley above Elan village, was mentioned in association with Arthur by Nennius in the tenth century. Near one of the cairns is a stone with a depression that looks like a paw print, said to be from one of Arthur's hounds (SN 9422 6442). Dinas Emrys (SH 606 492, literally the fortress of Ambrosius), near Beddgelert, is the place where Vortigern tried in vain to build a fortress, as described by Nennius and Geoffrey of Monmouth, but the building materials disappeared overnight, no matter how many times they were assembled. When it was discovered that there were two dragons sleeping under the site of the fortress Merlin explained that the red dragon stood for the Britons and the white dragon stood for the Saxons. Although the white dragon seemed the stronger, Merlin prophesied that the red dragon would eventually rise up and drive out the white dragon – the red dragon remains the symbol of Wales and is on the national flag. Elements of the story appear as a prequel in 'Lludd and Llefelys' in *The Mabinogion*, where one of three plagues blighting

An oval stone setting in the Preseli Hills (Pembrokeshire), probably prehistoric, is known as Bedd Arthur – one of many places in the landscape to have acquired Arthurian associations.

Bedd yr Afanc (Pembrokeshire) is the scant remains of a prehistoric chambered tomb, re-imagined as the grave of the legendary Afanc.

Britain is defeated by capturing the same two fighting dragons and burying them deep below Dinas Emrys.

Myths and legends are very adaptable. Most of those that have been preserved belong to recent centuries and were first collected in the nineteenth century, when folklorists believed that they belonged to time immemorial. The Afanc (which is also the Welsh word for beaver) was a water-dwelling monster who appears in Welsh mythology, mostly of nineteenth-century derivation, and was inevitably linked in with Arthurian legends. Bedd yr Afanc (SN 1079 3459), grave of the Afanc, is the remains of a Neolithic chambered tomb in the Preseli Hills in Pembrokeshire, but oddly where there is no large body of water. Otherwise it is lakes that the Afanc is associated with, like Llyn Barfog (or the 'bearded lake); above the Dyfi valley near Aberdyfi. It was here, according to latter-day lore, that the Afanc conspired to flood the neighbouring land (with a clear debt here to the Biblical flood), and could only be defeated by an acknowledged hero. Cue King Arthur, who dragged the beast from the lake, during which his horse left a hoof print on a nearby stone known as Carn Mach Arthur.

Arthurian legends might have become universal in Britain, but Owain Glyndŵr has remained exclusively Welsh. Owain led a rebellion against the English from 1400, during which he styled himself Prince of Wales and established a Welsh Parliament in Machynlleth. The mountains are important in the story of Owain. It was where he camped during the most successful part of his campaign; where he won his most famous victory; and, after establishing the parliament in Machynlleth, he retired to the mountains like the English kings retired to their palaces. The most important of the Welsh mountains to Owain was Plynlimon, which became an archetype of a mountainous stronghold. Owain Glyndŵr was on Plynlimon during the early, 'invincible' part of his rebellion. On Mynydd Hyddgen in 1401 Owain apparently led a small Welsh force to victory over a superior army. Early histories – the first account was written over a century after the events it was describing – recorded only 120 Welsh against 1,500 English and Flemish forces. Whether this battle really happened and whether the small Welsh contingent could have overcome such overwhelming odds has been a matter of debate for historians, but that is not what matters here. It established the Welsh mountains as an impregnable place of refuge for its people, a region that neither the English nor the Romans could really conquer.

The significance accorded to Owain Glyndŵr's supposed exploits on Plynlimon can be measured by the legends that have become attached to the place. Two blocks of white quartz by the Hyddgen, above Nant-y-Moch reservoir, known as Cerrig Cyfamod Glyndŵr ('stone of Glyndŵr's treaty'), are said to mark the place where Glyndŵr and Hugh Mortimer agreed to end hostilities (SN 7831 8964). Other features in the landscape have been interpreted as commemorating Owain's refuge in the hills. Glyndŵr was supposed to have slept, or perhaps sought refuge in a cave, possibly the cleft in the rock near Hyddgen known as Siambr Traws Fynydd. Craig y March (Rock of the Horse) is supposed to bear the hoof prints of Glyndŵr's horse, Llwyd y Bacsie; Cwm Gwarchae (Valley of the Siege) was supposed to have been so-named because Glyndŵr fought there.

The Chartist Cave near Llangynidr (SO 1277 1523) has become one of the focal points in commemoration of the Chartist rising of 1839, its mountain location symbolic of the nation's struggle. In this natural cave on a trackless moor, pikes and other weapons were stored in the summer of 1839 and were carried by the men of Tredegar in the march on Newport in November of that year. The event was pivotal in the fight for democratic rights in Britain, in which Wales played a prominent role, and was one of the most significant armed confrontations in nineteenth-century Britain, during which over 20 people were killed.

LANDSCAPE TOURISM

Place-names on a map are a record of how local communities saw their landscapes. But when did the rest of the world start to take notice of these self-contained, seemingly uneventful places? 'A vast wilderness, dismal to behold' was William Camden's verdict on the upper Wye in *Britannia*, published in 1586. In his account of British history, Vortigern, the foolish British king who invited the Saxons in, met his end in a lightning strike in the uplands above Rhayader, as if that is the sort of thing that happened to people in such places. William Camden was headmaster of Westminster School in London, so hardly the go-to person for insight on the remoter parts of Wales, but he was not the last of his ilk. There came a time (perhaps we are still in it) when upland Welsh communities were known to the wider world only through the lens of wealthy and time-rich people taking holidays.

Tourism in the landscapes of Wales began in the latter half of the eighteenth century. Most visitors were looking for picturesque scenery, but there was a fair sprinkling of geologists and botanists too, and it is also worth mentioning here the antiquaries Richard Fenton of Pembrokeshire, and Sir Richard Colt-Hoare of Stourhead in Wiltshire, who separately and together toured Wales in the early nineteenth century. A Celtic Grand Tour was popular at the end of the eighteenth and the beginning of the nineteenth century, in part because the European Grand Tour was out of bounds while Britain was at war with France. English tourists were fascinated with Welsh culture and places, seeing its ancient language, druids and bards as the equivalent in Britain of the heroic age to classical Greece. It was not long before itineraries became established. Most tourists followed established lowland routes on official roads (although excursions by boat down the lower Wye Valley were the most popular), but there were also summiteers who took on the likes of Yr Wyddfa, Cadair Idris and Plynlimon. This was serious business for some, like Joseph Hucks, who employed the services of a guide to ascend Cadair Idris in 1795, entrusting him with the necessary supplies for the journey – 'ham, fowl, bread, and cheese, and brandy'. Guides were common in the late-eighteenth and early-nineteenth century. In Dolgellau there were men who made a living from it, like Edward Roberts and Richard Pugh, but it was also possible to hire a local man, just as Thomas Turner did in 1840 when the landlord of the Blue Lion in Minffordd agreed to help him summit Cadair Idris.

The extensive literature of early travel employed a stock of ready-made emotions, vocabulary and reflexes, but people varied in their appreciation of the more remote parts of Wales (in some instances a reaction to the prevailing weather). Richard Warner, the Bath vicar who walked around Wales twice in the 1790s, noted of the road between Rhayader and Devil's Bridge, otherwise known as the 'Aberystwyth mountain road', that:

> No traces of human society appears, except in two or three small
> hovels, which occurred in the course of ten miles, and were
> inhabited by the joyless beings who tended the widely-spread
> flocks that fed upon these mountains. (1798, 61)

Perhaps he was tired, but if it was a difficult place to live, it could be a marvellous place to visit. On the same road three decades after Warner, Thomas Roscoe thought it was remote, but in a good way:

> A high, wide, swelling moorland, crowned in several places by
> carnau and tumuli, and extending around, far as the eye can reach,
> in one vast undulating waste, untenanted and uncultivated. The

The Aberystwyth mountain road in upland Ceredigion, in a desolate landscape that has variously been described as depressing and beautiful.

solitary grandeur of the scene is impressively beautiful, and the countless skylarks which people the clear air with their sweet voices, warbling their most eloquent music blithely around, add to the stern majesty of Nature her choicest melody.

By the time the Reverend Warner visited Eryri in 1797 there were local guides available for hire in Beddgelert. Having made the arduous ascent from Dinas Emrys with his guide William Lloyd, with only a 'leathern' bottle of milk for refreshment, Warner was a bit put out to encounter the 'hyperborean climate' of dense mist, until a short break allowed him to see just how precipitous the summit was. An alternative was to follow rivers to their sources, and for this the chief attraction was Plynlimon. Plynlimon may no longer be a magnet for hill walkers, but in the past it was sought after as the fountainhead of Wales, where the Severn, Wye and Rheidol rise within a few miles of each other. In Victorian Britain the impulse to reach the source of the Severn was the same as the impulse to find the source of the Nile. George Borrow, in 1854, was one of a number of walkers who ascended Plynlimon in search of the source of these great British rivers, insisting on drinking from each of them.

By the early twentieth century all classes of society were able to take holidays. The social elite visited shooting estates for country sports, while for the working classes and the spiritually minded this was the age of the wayfarer or rambler. Organisations like the Co-operative and Communal Holidays Fellowship, which had a hostel near Conwy by 1913, allowed workmen and their families to take open-air holidays in the Welsh mountains. The Youth Hostels Association was founded in 1930 and its first hostel was at Pennant Hall, Llanrwst. Idwal Cottae, Nant Ffrancon, is now the longest-serving hostel in Wales, opened in 1931. The commercial potential of mass tourism in the mountains had been recognised and exploited earlier. There were wooden huts around the summit of Yr Wyddfa in the nineteenth century, and a hotel by the end of the century. Plans to build a railway to the summit were originally resisted by the landowner, Thomas Assheton Smith, but when the North Wales Narrow Gauge Railway (now the Welsh Highland Railway) reached the south-west foot of the mountain, at Rhyd-du, in 1881 it took some of the tourist trade away from Llanberis and so Assheton Smith had a change of heart. The Yr Wyddfa Mountain Railway was built between 1894 and 1896 and used locomotives built in Switzerland. The old summit buildings were replaced in 1930 by a new building designed by Clough Williams-Ellis, but this coped poorly with the challenging weather conditions and was itself replaced by Ray Hole's Hafod Eryri in 2007. No one now summits Yr Wyddfa in search of peace and solitude.

Creation of open access land in 2000 under the Countryside and Rights of Way Act was the culmination of several decades of managing the hills as a place of recreation. The National Parks and Access to the Countryside Act was passed in 1949. Eryri was designated a National Park in 1951, followed by the Pembrokeshire Coast (including the Preseli Hills) in 1952, and Bannau Brycheiniog in 1957. The weakness

The Jubilee Pillars were set up in 1888 to mark the start of a 'Jubilee Walk' for visitors staying at the nearby resort of Penmaenmawr (Conwy).

Wind farms above the Wye Valley, in the uplands of Central Wales, have been built where National Park status failed at the last hurdle.

of the Act was that it covered large areas of upland, leaving smaller areas unprotected. This prompted the creation of a similar designation, Areas of Outstanding Natural Beauty (AONB), the first of which to be designated was the Gower peninsula in 1956. This was followed in Wales by the Llŷn Peninsula and the Clwydian Hills, which include extensive upland landscapes. Areas of Outstanding Natural Beauty are similar to National Parks, but they do not have the planning restrictions of the latter. Another offshoot of the National Parks movement was the creation of Long Distance Paths, now known as National Trails, of which Offa's Dyke and Glyndŵr's Way, to name just two, pass over upland landscapes.

However, these designations cover only a small proportion of the Welsh mountains. If you look at a contour map of Britain, where the high ground is shaded brown, it is striking that most of it is within National Parks, but that the central mountainous area of Wales is omitted. For this there is a purely political reason. A proposal for a Cambrian Mountains National Park was first put forward in 1965, and in 1972 the Countryside Commission issued the necessary designation order. But there was considerable opposition from local authorities and farmers, sufficient for the Secretary of State for Wales to refuse confirmation of the order. So there was to be no National Park. Two significant consequences of this are that the footfall in these hills is much less than in the National Parks, which are much better known and celebrated, and the Cambrian Mountains has more than its fair share of wind turbines. But it was also a push-back against the assumption that future management of these hills should be decided in cities. It is some compensation that the Cambrian Mountains are now designated as a dark-sky park and have become an important leisure destination around the Elan Valley reservoirs.

Mountains are a key element in Welsh national identity, which in the Welsh mind are seen perhaps as inalienable repositories of Welshness, safe from outside influence and a part of Wales that has never really been conquered by outsiders, either military generals or mine captains. If so, recent history has challenged that assumption. Rural depopulation has eroded local communities. Resentment has been felt over significant landscape change. Abandoned farmland was turned over to forestry in the early twentieth century, partly to provide rural employment but also to solve the nation's perceived shortfall in timber production; wind turbines have spoiled the view in the eyes of

The former Bryntail Lead Mine has been restored and interpreted, and stands in the shadow of Llyn Clywedog reservoir dam above Llanidloes.

many people and the flooding of upland river valleys to create reservoirs has displaced local people. It is notable that the emergence of the Welsh nationalist movement in the twentieth century grew not out of Cardiff, Aberystwyth, Caernarfon or Bangor, but from the flooding of a sparsely populated upland valley north of Bala called Tryweryn.

Ruined houses document the decline of the upland population in modern times. A miner's cottage at Drws y Coed in Eryri National Park.

2

BOUNDARIES

ALL land in Wales is owned by someone, regardless of any right to roam, and has been since at least the medieval period. When land is of precious value or its ownership has been contested, owners have been quick to define their boundaries, which are expressed in various ways across the landscape. In lowland landscapes, ownership boundaries are also boundaries of land use, like field walls or hedges, but on the open hills different ways are needed to define boundaries over large tracts of ground.

No definite prehistoric boundaries have been identified across the landscapes of Wales, and so archaeological evidence begins with the re-ordering of the political landscape after the end of Roman administration. The best-known feature of land division in Wales is Offa's Dyke, which defined the boundary of the Mercian kingdom – what is now the English Midlands – from Powys and Monmouthshire in Wales. But there are numerous shorter dykes, helpfully known as short dykes or cross dykes, that also probably acted as boundary markers. Short dykes are linear banks found in the uplands in eastern and south-east Wales and across the border in England, but are less common in north-west Wales. They have long been associated with Offa's Dyke along with the presumption that their purpose was similar, or even that they were part of the same defensive system. They are thought to have been raised from the eighth to the tenth centuries, based on the date of Offa's Dyke, but they rarely yield any archaeological evidence that confirms this. The precise functions of short dykes are debated and many have been interpreted as route blockers designed to deter raiders from the east because they are often built across ridgeways. This interpretation has been influenced by that other great defensive barrier in Britain, Hadrian's Wall. But Hadrian's Wall was garrisoned with troops who could monitor hostile movements from watch towers. Short dykes have no such infrastructure and there is no evidence that they were manned. As defensive features they are unlikely to have presented a very formidable barrier. In most cases it would have been easy for an invading force to outflank them or simply walk over the top of them. As prominent landscape features it would be surprising if they did not figure as ownership boundaries, even if that was not their original purpose. In the twelfth-century *Book of Llandaf,* boundaries are usually described as banks or ditches (or natural features). And so it is more likely that they defined boundaries, perhaps of the Welsh

Two Tumps Dyke crosses the summit of Kerry Hill and crosses the headwaters of the rivers Teme and Mule in the Montgomeryshire district of Powys. Although about 700m long in total, the earthwork is not continuous and it is not certain that it ever was.

administrative units known as *cantrefs*, or perhaps they delineated land holdings where livestock could be grazed.

How can you spot a short dyke? Firstly, it should be remembered that dyke is not a very accurate description. These linear earthworks are made up of a bank and a ditch (and sometimes even double banks). Short dykes were constructed as a single feature, unlike most later field boundaries which are part of a system. In the valleys of South Wales they can be seen to cross ridges laterally. The place-name to look out for is *Clawdd*, which is often used to describe a bank and/or ditch. They are easiest to identify where they cross open moorland because they are substantial structures but are clearly not part of a wider complex of earthworks.

Substantial boundaries were a feature of medieval monastic estates but there is little evidence to be found in the uplands. The best-known is Clawdd Seri (SH 4168 4643) on the Llŷn Peninsula, in the form of a bank and ditch over 1km long across an open landscape between two marshy areas. It is mentioned in a charter of Aberconwy Abbey of *c*.1200, where its established name suggests that it is of earlier origin. Another good example of a boundary bank is at Waen Blaen Lliw (SH 7997 3518), west of Moel Llyfnant in Merioneth, which probably defined the upper limit of a monastic grange, but was also the boundary between the enclosed pasture and the open mountain.

Boundaries across mountain land are uncommon in the Middle Ages, perhaps because there was more than enough for the resident population to make use of. It helps to explain why it may seem counter-intuitive to search out evidence of land ownership in the hills. It may also explain why there is a natural tendency to think of mountain land as common land. Although there are some pockets of common land in Wales it is a myth that it refers to 'common ownership', when in fact it refers to common rights of access and use. The concept as we understand it today was imported from England at the time of the Act of Union between England and Wales, that was passed in 1536. It largely concerns 'wastes', a term with misleading connotations of uselessness, but that really means uncultivated or unenclosed pasture, which covers both mountain land as well as difficult terrain like bogs and marshes. However, access to mountain land in earlier times was well established in Wales. In the late 1530s John Leland found that all of the mountain land between Strata Florida Abbey and the Elan Valley was used as wild pasture by all the inhabitants in the vicinity, for which they paid no rent. Rights to exploit these upland resources in the post-medieval centuries were limited by parish boundaries. So we are talking about local rights, not universal rights. Common rights allowed commoners to graze animals (*pasture*), dig peat (*turbary*), take wood (*estover*), to fish from streams or ponds (*piscary*) and to dig for sand, gravel, coal, stone and minerals. Many of these activities have left their mark on the landscape and we will encounter them later.

The extent of unenclosed mountain land has diminished significantly over the past three centuries. Enclosure in the uplands created private holdings on land that was previously waste. In most cases this was the result of a Parliamentary Act, organised on a parish basis, but we will find many examples of illegal settlers, or squatters, who established holdings on marginal wastes that have had the long-term consequence of remaining in private hands and excluded from the right to roam.

Boundaries became more important in the age of leisure and during the industrial revolution when the value of mineral deposits below ground became the chief value of many upland landholdings. The growth of mining and quarrying in the nineteenth century affected most of the uplands of Wales, bringing monetary significance to land that was once of little value – and large fortunes to people like the second Marquess of Bute in South Wales, the Assheton Smiths and the Lords Penrhyn in North Wales. The other main development was the establishment of shooting estates in the nineteenth century.

Unlike most archaeological features in the uplands, which record a way of life of upland people in general, evidence of land ownership is dedicated to certain individuals, who were not necessarily local residents. By the nineteenth century they were often incomers who had made their fortune in trade and craved the country estate and its 'old

An unworked stone on the hills above Penmaenmawr marks the boundary between Llanfairfechan and Dwygyfylchi parishes, where there were common grazing rights.

money' connotations as a mark of status. The physical evidence in the landscape for land ownership is therefore usually some form of boundary marker.

Boundaries are often marked by natural features like streams, or prominent archaeological features like prehistoric cairns, many of which occupy natural boundaries such as hilltop ridges. Special boundary markers come mainly in two forms – piles of stones and upright stones. These are usually marked on the county-series Ordnance Survey maps published from the 1870s onwards, though piles of stones are not marked as antiquities in order to distinguish them from genuine prehistoric remains.

Boundary stones are uprights, usually unworked, possibly (but not necessarily) carved with the initials of the landowners, often on both sides. The stones can easily be mistaken for prehistoric stones (and in some cases *are* prehistoric stones with initials carved on them), and many of them can be found lying flat on the ground. These markers rarely exist in isolation, but were part of a series of markers placed at regular intervals on the boundary. In North Wales it is common to find stones marked 'WWW', referring to several generations of the family bearing the name Sir Watkin Williams-Wynn, of which the third generation (1772–1840), and fourth baronet, referred to himself as the 'Prince in Wales'. The family had the largest land holding in North Wales.

Accurate ownership boundaries have for a long time been determined by maps, the earliest of which were bespoke surveys of individual estates. The Ordnance Survey was established in the early nineteenth century to map the whole of Great Britain and it started surveying detailed maps in the second half of the nineteenth century. It made its direct mark on the landscape during efforts to map rapid

Sir Watkin Williams-Wynn owned the largest landholding in North Wales and his boundary stones are a frequent sight on the open hillsides. (Image taken during a survey for the RCAHMW)

An unworked monolith with a cast-iron plate marks the boundary of the earl of Dudley's estate in the Berwyn Mountains near Bala. Plantations in Jamaica and mineral rights in the Black Country provided the wealth to purchase an estate in Wales.

changes in the British landscape in the decades after the First World War. From 1936, the familiar triangulation pillars, or trig points, were installed, mostly on hilltops; every one of which is intervisible with at least two others, assuming it is a fine day. The tapering concrete pillars, designed by Brigadier Martin Hotine, have a brass fitting on the top for attaching a theodolite. By careful measurement of the angles between these trig points, the exact positions of roads and field walls, mountain tops and watercourses could be plotted in a method known as triangulation. Increasingly obsolete since the development of aerial and satellite images, they still have a role in guiding hikers to what are always good viewpoints. And for the more agile among us standing on top of them has become a rite of passage.

A small nineteenth-century boundary stone in the Berwyn Mountains. Its weathered inscription is now barely legible but refers to the land owned by Anna Maria Mynne of nearby Llandrillo (Denbighshire).

One of a line of unworked quartz boundary markers on the Preseli Hills (Pembrokeshire)

3

ROADS AND TRACKS

THE Right to Roam legislation that was introduced in 2000 gives us the right to walk wherever we want over the uplands, but in practice we all tend to follow existing paths. Going off the beaten track is in many places very difficult, and when we do, because we tend to follow the line of least resistance, we often end up just following sheep or tractor tracks. Fortunately the uplands are covered by roads, tracks, bridleways and footpaths, all of which have a historical dimension. To follow any of them is therefore to follow in other people's footsteps and to experience the landscape as history. The most well-used ways are marked as bridleways or pathways on the Ordnance Survey map, but these routes can date from just about any period, from prehistory to recent centuries. How deep into history any single road or path goes is often much more difficult to tell, even if the majority of them are probably relatively recent.

Roads can often be dated only by the structures associated with them. This is certainly true of prehistoric routes, which will undoubtedly have changed in form if they are still in use. An added difficulty of identifying prehistoric roads is that we rarely know the start and end points of journeys. One end of a prehistoric route appears to have been the Graig Lwyd axe factories on the hill above Penmaenmawr. The track running eastwards from the quarries, now designated as part of the North Wales Path, has numerous significant Bronze Age monuments centred around the Druids Circle (SH 7228 7465). So it

A prehistoric route above the Conwy Valley, later a Roman road, now looks like any other post-medieval track, but several Bronze Age monuments line this section of road.

was clearly a prehistoric route, but it is the associated monuments that define it rather than any intrinsic quality of the existing path.

Single standing stones have often been interpreted as having been set up along prehistoric routes. They show activity along the line of a route, and their frequency may give some indication of the importance of the route, but they can hardly have been set up as signposts. Five standing stones line a route south-westwards from Moel Goedog to the coast at Llanbedr near Harlech, now a minor road (the northernmost at SH 6071 3204). Although they are nicely spread out over a distance of about 1.5km, the largest of the stones is over 2m tall and is unlikely to have been moved very far. On the high plateau between the Conwy Valley and Bangor there is a prehistoric route with five standing stones (and a stone circle) over a distance of nearly 3km, but in this case very unevenly distributed. Again, their size suggests that the tallest of them cannot have travelled far (they are much larger than the relatively small megaliths transported from Pembrokeshire to Stonehenge). It is equally the case that where standing stones are found on known pre-historic routes, cairns are just as likely also to be found.

The practice of erecting monuments along established routes continued into historic times. The presence of stones which can be dated
to the early medieval period, from the fifth century onwards, helps to
identify routes that were in use at that time. Maen Madoc (SN 9187
1578) is an early-medieval inscribed stone beside the Roman road (Sarn
Helen) between Brecon and Neath. The Ponsticill (or Cwm Criban)
inscribed stone (SO 0726 1317), an early-medieval inscribed stone with
Ogham script, stands beside a well-defined trackway along the Cefn-
yr-Ystrad ridge toward Ponsticill on the Taf Fechan river.

However, it is easier to identify roads from the Roman period, and
when we talk of Roman roads we mean military roads. They were
devised to provide a network for efficient communication between
forts, which were established during the first century AD to consoli-
date Roman control of the region, including its uplands. A reliable road,
combined with forts manned with auxiliary troops, had the secondary
effects of stimulating trade, creating a new economic pattern across the
nation and making the exploitation of raw materials more feasible.

A section of Sarn Helen, beside which is the early-medieval stone known
as Maen Madoc, is now reduced to a farm track.

The Roman roads over upland terrain are not normally straight. Instead, the course of the road is dictated by the lie of the land: with the roads constructed in a series of straight sections, as long as the terrain will allow, with zig-zag sections on the steepest ground. Where Roman roads have been incorporated into modern roads there is often no obvious evidence of their origin. However, excavation of sections of Roman roads in the uplands suggests that they were simpler than lowland roads, but nevertheless were well constructed, about 4–5m wide, with shallow ditches on either side. They were built as raised aggers, or sometimes as terraces, with flanking ditches to allow drainage. The metalling of the roads consisted of crushed stones which were obtained locally. On upland sections there is often a line of small quarry pits along the course of the road, from where the road surface was obtained – a more commonly visible sign that a road is of Roman origin. Some sections of road were laid with slabs, which have been uncovered during excavations. These appear to have been used sparingly on upland roads, perhaps confined to places where slabs were easily available, or where the ground was poorly drained.

Perhaps the best example of how a Roman road became a defining feature in later culture is Sarn Helen – the road, or series of roads, between Canovium fort at Caerhun in the Conwy Valley and Carmarthen. As a single entity Sarn Helen is a medieval idea rather than a Roman one. The story of its origin is found in *The Mabinogion*, in the tale of the Emperor Maxen, or Maxen Wledig, and probably referring to Magnus Maximus, the Roman commander who was proclaimed Emperor by his own men in AD 383, but who was later executed in AD 388. Maxen's bride was Helen, or Elen, who ordered the building of a road between her strongholds at Segontium (near Caernarfon) and Carmarthen. Many of the Roman roads between these two places of course traverse lowland territory, but there are upland stretches too, some of them well preserved. These include sections near Tomen-y Mur Roman fort (SH 7096 3970), above the Lledr valley near Dolwyddelan (SH 7603 5453) and an especially well-preserved section in the hills east of Trawsfynydd (SH 7266 3190).

Major upland routes of the medieval period are likely to be associated with pilgrimage, the needs of the monasteries or were drovers' routes. Penrhys, on the hill between the two Rhondda valleys, is known now as a 1960s hilltop village, but it had a hilltop shrine and was a significant centre of pilgrimage by the fifteenth century. Part of the approach to the shrine from the south is still discernible as a ridgeway track (ST 002 946).

The Monk's Trod is, arguably, one of the best-preserved medieval routes in Britain. It crosses the Cambrian Mountains between the Cistercian monasteries of Strata Florida (Ceredigion) and Abbey Cwmhir (Powys), with a further branch to Strata Marcella near Welshpool (also Powys). It was probably created in the 1170s, soon after the monasteries were founded, and may have been the road taken by Gerald of Wales when he 'hastened' over the mountains of Elenydd in 1199. It was a useful link between these important monastic houses, and gave access to granges (farms) on Strata Florida's estates. It was also useful politically for the Welsh rulers, such as the Lord Rhys (Rhys ap Gruffudd) and Llywelyn Fawr, to maintain control and communications over a large territory to counter the rival Marcher lords to the east. The fact that no road or railway builder has ever repeated such an upland route as an important artery of communication shows how the political geography of Wales has changed over the centuries.

The Monk's Trod crosses bleak and largely featureless moorland in the Cambrian Mountains (Ceredigion and Powys). Some of the surviving sections have probably been widened by the use of farm vehicles.

It was never called the Monk's Trod, needless to say, which is probably just a fanciful name conjured by antiquaries.

Although it begins near the head of the Teifi river, where the water flows westwards, the Monk's Trod soon crosses to terrain near the head of the Claerwen, from where the water flows eastwards, destined eventually for the River Wye. The upland section of the road, from near to the Teifi Pools on the west side to the River Wye on the east side, can be followed quite easily for long sections, and is mostly still a public right of way. Until the nineteenth century it was a drovers' road. The sections easiest to identify are where the track has been cut into the hillside to create a terrace. The road crosses Afon Claerwen, above the reservoir of the same name, at Rhyd Hengae (SN 8238 6820), and between here and the crossing of the Elan to the north-east is a long section of over 8km that is well preserved. Uphill from Rhyd Hengae, the surface appears to have been roughly cobbled. Where the road crosses the Elan river it intersects with the Aberystwyth mountain road, but takes a different course. One branch leads north towards Strata Marcella on the Severn, but the main road continues on over moorland to the River Wye. It crosses a stream at Rhyd Garreg-lwyd (SN 9230 7161), where there are remains of two former slab bridges, of unknown date but probably associated with the later history of the road. These would have been used by horses and pack animals rather than carts. An alternative course of the road crosses Maen Serth Ridge and descends to the Wye nearer Rhayader. This route is also clearly defined and along its course is the stone known as Maen Serth, marked with a cross (SN 9430 6988).

The road has many of the physical features associated with other upland roads. Part of it is cut into bedrock, there is evidence that it has had a metalled surface, and there are small patches where paving stones have survived. In parts, where the ground is level and feature-less, there are no physical traces of the road at all. In a small section where it passes on the north side of the modern Craig Goch reservoir it is overlain by the mountain road between Aberystwyth and Rhayader, and close by is another section more or less obliterated by a

Pont Scethin is an isolated but well-constructed arched bridge of field stone, on an inland route from Dyffryn Ardudwy (Gwynedd).

bulldozer-formed track that overlies it. Such is the fate of roads, and the problems of identifying their age.

In the Ardudwy district of Eryri the mountains are a formidable barrier between the coastal plain and inland Merioneth. The routes over the mountain declined in the nineteenth century when the turn-pike road and the railway chose to follow the coastline from Harlech to Barmouth and Dolgellau. Before that, Harlech, Dyffryn Ardudwy, Llanbedr and other settlements were relatively isolated from the remainder of Wales, although we should not forget the importance of coastal shipping in the pre-railway era. Several notable tracks cross the mountainous terrain of Rhinog from west to east, including the Roman Steps, Bwlch Drws Ardudwy and the drovers' route to Dolgellau. From Dyffryn Ardudwy the drovers route leads across the moors, much of it with enclosed pasture on the west side, to the pack-horse bridge known as Pont Scethin, a well-built structure that is tes-tament to the importance of the overland route towards Dolgellau (SH 6344 2354). The 'Roman Steps' are not Roman at all, but a medieval packhorse route that has been, and remains, substantially paved, with slabs laid or arches built across the streams it traverses (SH 64953057).

The Roman Steps is a packhorse route across the Rhinog (Gwynedd), partly paved and with small bridges over numerous streams, of simple arched construction or just plain slabs.

Droving began in the medieval period, whereby herds of cattle would be driven eastwards from Wales to England to be sold in markets as far as London and Kent; however, most of the evidence associated with them is later. A team of drovers and their corgis would drive up to 400 animals along established routes, often avoiding main roads, covering up to a dozen miles a day. It could take three weeks to drive the animals to market. Upland sections of drovers' routes have little to identify them. However, tangible evidence of the drovers route across Mynydd Epynt is marked by former drovers inns, their positions sealed after the area was requisitioned for military training in 1939. They include Tafarn-y-Mynydd (SN 9187 4225) and The Drovers Arms (SN 9860 4510).

Upland roads were used for local travel and were not fit for purpose when the tourists arrived in the eighteenth century. The general consensus was that the state of roads in rural Wales, and especially in the uplands, was appalling as late as 1800. Taking the road from

Ffynnon Eidda, dated 1846, is a rare example in the uplands of roadside water provided for animals driven across the hills near Penmachno (Conwy). Exactly how it was used is not clear because there is no trough for animals to drink from and the chamber itself is not accessible to animals.

Bala over the pass at Bwlch-y-Groes, Arthur Aikin wrote in 1797 of a 'miserably rugged road of loose slates, rendered slippery by the rain which was coming down with increasing violence'. Others quite enjoyed the danger of this rugged mountain pass, although the prevailing weather was clearly a factor. Richard Fenton encountered it in August 1808 as a 'tolerable road' leading up to the pass from Dinas Mawddwy. Descending toward Bala on the other side it had become 'a very formidable road, without a parapet on one side, and on the other a high mountain of shivering slate'. Maintenance of roads was the responsibility of the parish, who usually had little incentive and, in upland regions, few resources, to devote to road improvement. William Williams of Llandegai, writing in 1802 about the road from Beddgelert to Capel Curig, remarked that 'it is much to be regretted, that Gentlemen who have property in this and other such vales, are so indifferent and inattentive, that they do not open a communication with the country by means of new and safe roads'. The poor state of the roads was a drag on the local economy. Williams argued that a decent road from the Llŷn Peninsula to Llanrwst in the Conwy Valley, over the mountains between Beddgelert and Betws-y-Coed, would be a more convenient way of transporting produce from one of the richest farming districts of North Wales than the route by sea. This said, the route would be improved partly by Thomas Telford's Holyhead Road in the early nineteenth century, but was not fully realised until the County Council took over responsibility for the highway in the late-nineteenth century.

The immediate solution to the problem of poor roads was the creation of turnpike trusts, established by separate Acts of Parliament between 1652 and 1752. They brought significant improvements to major routes, at the price of a toll for using them, but few of these crossed over upland terrain. There were also private roads, like the road built by Lord Penrhyn from Bangor to Capel Curig at the end of the eighteenth century, which has survived as an unmodernised track since it was superseded in 1815 by the Holyhead Road, built by Thomas Telford, from London to Holyhead. This passes over the high ground

The old road from Capel Curig to Bangor was built by the Penrhyn Estate but was superseded when Thomas Telford's Holyhead Road opened in 1815, running parallel with the old road on the opposite side of the Llugwy Valley.

between Betws-y-Coed and Bethesda, by way of Capel Curig. After their formation in 1889 the county councils assumed responsibility for the road network and were largely responsible for the network of major and minor roads that exists today.

Milestones, which are not often found in upland landscapes, are an indicator of when roads were improved. There are milestones on turnpike roads: for example, the unworked monoliths alongside the Aberystwyth mountain road. Thomas Telford's Holyhead Road retains its original mile markers, even on the higher ground, which are of cast iron plates set into stone. There are also many mile markers, typically of cast iron or dressed stone, on roads maintained from the late-nineteenth century by the County Councils.

Post-medieval roads, including roads constructed and maintained by Turnpike Trusts, have some different characteristics to Roman roads, but are in many ways quite similar – the same general width, and with similar metalled surfaces. But there are some significant differences. Retaining walls, stone revetments to raised sections of causeway, rock-cut

TOP: The road between Capel Curig and Beddgelert was improved after it became the responsibility of the County Council in 1889. Its milestones date from this period. BOTTOM LEFT: This milestone on the Aberystwyth mountain road was put up probably in the late-eighteenth century when it became a turnpike road. BOTTOM RIGHT: Thomas Telford's Holyhead Road has a well-preserved sequence of milestones.

or otherwise sunken sections, as well as wider roads, are all indications of a later date. Likewise, although Roman roads had culverts for drainage, any surviving examples are likely to belong to recent centuries.

Another sign that a road or an upland track was formerly a road of some importance is the presence of a named stream or river crossing. The place-name *rhyd* is common in upland Wales and refers to a ford. Sometimes the place-name has remained after the ford has been superseded by a bridge (as at Pont Rhyd Galed in the Upper Wye Valley). In Eryri there are 'Roman bridges' that are, in reality, from the post-medieval centuries. Until the nineteenth century most bridges in Wales were built of timber, but in the uplands stone was easily available and timber was not. The simplest form was to lay a slab over a stream. For wider streams at least one upright was needed mid-stream, over which slabs (clappers) were laid. So there are early upland stone bridges even though most crossings were still forded.

Clues to roads, tracks and paths can also be found by looking at Ordnance Survey maps. In Radnorshire there are many designated public footpaths to the uplands that simply cease, seemingly without reason. But close examination of the old Ordnance Survey maps reveals that these were paths to now-vanished cottages built on the commons. The rights of way shown on the Ordnance Survey maps show paths and tracks that were in use when the rights of way were established definitively in the twentieth century. The Highways Act of 1835 established that rights of way – on roads, cartways, bridleways and pathways – were part of 'the King's Highway', in other words, public passage for use by everybody. However, the Ordnance Survey did not include information on public rights of way until the 1960s, by which time local authorities were required to maintain definitive records of them. Many old tracks had fallen out of use by then. It is not uncommon to find evidence of a former homestead or *hafoty*, but no evidence of a path or track that leads to it.

A path is not a permanent fixture on the landscape. The rights of way marked on an Ordnance Survey map therefore only show those paths and bridleways that existed when the definitive maps were prepared.

This Eryri quarry road is typical of post-medieval upland roads over difficult terrain, requiring a raised track retained by a stone wall.

When George Borrow visited Plynlimon in the 1850s he was taken up there by a local guide. The route they took from the inn at Dyffryn Castell is still a public footpath, but once on top of Plynlimon Fawr, the paths that Borrow walked on have now disappeared. Borrow was guided to the lake at the source of the Rheidol on a path that the guide warned him was 'more fit for sheep or shepherds than gentle-folk', then walked to the source of the Severn, and then a 15-minute walk to the source of the Wye. This route is no longer practical in an upland land-scape where there are no rights of way and where the terrain is slow going (the Wye Valley walk was created before the Right to Roam leg-islation was passed, and does not even start at the source of the Wye, to which there are no footpaths).

As a general rule, the more recent a pathway or track was created, the more likely we are to be able to explain it. The clue is always in associated structures. There are upland paths and tracks that workmen trod to mine workings and quarries. Every year thousands of walk-ers approach Yr Wyddfa via the Miners' Track from Pen-y-pass to the former Britannia Copper Mine by Glaslyn (SH 6202 5457), which worked from the eighteenth century until 1916, on the way passing the barracks in which the workmen lodged for the week (SH 6415 5483). Other tracks lead to or pass sheepfolds, and were used by shepherds gaining access to sheep walks. Tracks that lead on to moorland and then peter out might be the only visible indication of an area of former peat cuttings. Other tracks might have led to homesteads, or alternatively the *hafotai*, or summer dwellings.

The expansion of mining and quarrying from the eighteenth century brought with it new demands for improved transport infrastructure. Many of the tracks across upland terrain were associated with these industries, and many of them are the lines of old railways. Before the advent of tramroads and railways, however, the most primitive mode of transport was the use of horse-drawn sleds, similar to sleds laden with peat used by farmers for descending steep ground, which are described in a later chapter. But the most favoured form was the packhorse. Packhorse routes were needed to transport what were usually heavy and bulky goods mined and quarried in the uplands. This applies especially to the small quarry and mine workings in the early phases of metal mining in mid Wales, and slate quarrying in North Wales. Pack animals could carry loads in wicker panniers slung over the backs of the animals, and in the North Wales slate quarries usually worked in trains. The footpath from Cwm Penmachno to the former Rhiwbach Quarry (SH 741 462), now part of the Eryri Slate Trail, is an old drovers' route that was taken over as a packhorse route when the quarry was first worked in the eighteenth century, and was later the route taken by workmen who walked up the steep hill from the village until the quarry finally closed in 1953.

Carts began to supersede pack animals in the slate industry after 1800, hauled by two horses, with sometimes a third attached to the rear of the cart to act as a brake. Contemporary paintings show this system in use at Dinorwic in 1795, when the slates were transported down the precipitous 'drag' to boats moored on Llyn Peris. Several cart roads were built in Eryri in the early nineteenth century, before narrow-gauge railways had come into being. To follow them on foot is to understand just how isolated many of these quarries were as the economy and scale of the slate industry was beginning to gather pace. Ffordd yr Iuddew Mawr (road of the Great Jew) was built in the 1820s by John Rogers of Wrexham for the Royal Cambrian Company. It served the Moelwyn quarries, now partially submerged under the Llyn Stwlan reservoir. The road is now a 1½-mile public footpath on the west side of Moelwyn Bach (SH 6500 4994), linking a minor road near Croesor with Bwlch Stwlan. At the summit is an extension of the 1850s road, known as the Pant Mawr road (SH 657 444), which is well engineered across a steep slope that heads northwards to the former Pant Mawr slate quarry.

Cart roads were superseded by railroads in the early nineteenth century in the slate districts of North Wales, but the transition had already occurred in South Wales, especially for transporting iron ore and coal to the ironworks. The form of these railroads varied considerably. Known as tramways (sometimes also as plateways) these had L-shaped iron plates bolted to stone setts in the ground. The wheels rested on the bottom of the plate and were kept in place by the vertical section of the tramway plate. Survival of the original iron plates is extremely rare but there are many places where lines of the stone setts have survived. In the slate districts of North Wales the most common method was to have the wheels on top of the rail, and to be kept in place by a flange on the wheel. This is, of course, standard practice on the world's railways. But, although there was a standard gauge for

Stone setts are all that distinguishes this muddy track as a former tramroad, part of the Brecon Forest Tramroad.

railways of 4 feet 8½ inches, the gauges of industrial railways were usually narrower, such as the common 2-foot gauge. The larger slate quarries of the nineteenth century also had internal railway systems and their former presence is indicated by the runs to the large finger tips that have become a characteristic feature of the slate landscape. Horse-drawn tramways pre-dated standard-gauge railways and were also used in more challenging terrain, where their narrow gauge and simpler engineering made them more economical. The narrow-gauge railways for which Wales has become famous grew out of the quarry railroads, and were used for both passenger traffic and the transport of bulky materials.

However, on the ground, how can you tell the difference between a tramway or railway, and a track or path? Of course old tramway and railroad lines have since become tracks and paths, but there are various distinguishing features in their design. If it has sharp bends it is more likely to be a track or a tramway, but not a standard-gauge railway, which needs a wider turning circle. One of the easiest ways to distinguish between a track and a railway or tramway is if it follows

The line of the Bwlch y Rhosydd railway, built in 1864, led from the slate mines along a level rock-cut terrace to the incline that descended into Cwm Croesor (Gwynedd).

The imprint of railway sleepers indicates the line of a former railway at the Trefor Rocks quarry (Denbighshire).

a steep gradient it is a track. Railways and tramways were engineered to follow as level a course as possible. If significant changes in altitude were required, the most common way of solving this was by means of an inclined plane.

Inclined planes are among the more striking of industrial remains in the landscape and are associated with tramways and railways. The technology allowed goods to be transported over steeper terrain than was possible using road transport, and often required building substantial stone retaining walls to support an even track bed. They were known in western Britain from the seventeenth century, when they were used to lower coal from pits to wharfs on the River Severn in Shropshire.

Examples in upland Wales belong to the nineteenth century and are associated with stone and slate quarrying and ironworking. Most inclined planes were operated by the principle of counterbalancing, allowing empty wagons to be hauled up on one of the tracks while laden wagons were lowered down on the other track. At the top there were parallel walls to which the horizontal winding drum was fixed by means of timber beams, and perhaps also a small hut from which the process was controlled by a brakeman who could hand-operate the brake callipers, which had wooden brake blocks. The winding houses are easy to identify because they stand at the top of the incline, in line with the track bed, although it was not necessary to provide a roof over the drums, and in some cases the winding drums were exposed to the elements. Although ropes were initially made of hemp, surviving examples are iron or steel cables, and it is quite common to find a length of it embedded in the ground at or by an old incline. If motive power was needed, this was achieved by a horse whim, whereby a horse wound rope around a drum by walking in a circle, or latterly by means of waterwheels, steam engines, diesel or electric motors. The most ingenious method is perhaps the water-balance incline, whereby the load to be lowered down the incline was counterbalanced by a tank of water on a separate wagon. These devices were adapted from their use as vertical lifts in the shafts of coal mines, where they were used in the early nineteenth century in shallow self-draining coal pits. There were several examples in the North Wales slate quarries, and one at Pwll Du limestone quarry near Blaenavon (SO 2514 1146). (The technology remains in use today for cliff railways, such as the Lynmouth-Lynton Railway in North Devon, and the lift to the main site at the Centre for Alternative Technology near Machynlleth.)

Hill's Tramroad opened in 1821 to serve the Blaenavon Ironworks. It was engineered from Pwll Du around the north side of the Blorenge, from where there are inclined planes down to the level of the Brecknock and Abergavenny Canal. It had a narrow gauge, only 2 feet wide, and took materials to and from Blaenavon Ironworks, and from the nearby mines and quarries. There is even a tunnel close to the Pwll Du quarry,

The inclined plane at Rhosydd slate quarry (Gwynedd).

The winding house at Bryn Glas Quarry incline, near Llan Ffestiniog (Gwynedd), was built in the 1890s.

Fragments of machinery are often found at the ruins of inclined planes.

The line of Hill's Tramroad (Monmouthshire) is cut into the site of a steep valley side known as The Tumble.

but the distinguishing feature is its rock-cut course on the side of a steep hill, and sections where stone setts have survived. The tramroad passes the Garnddyrys Forge, from where bar iron was transported, but the tramroad was also used to transport pig iron from the main Blaenavon Ironworks, coal from local pits and limestone for the canalside lime kilns. It continued working until the 1870s.

A different, more speculative enterprise was the Brecon Forest Tramroad. Built in the 1820s by the landowner John Christie, a successful London indigo trader, it was intended to supply limestone to the iron industry, and lime for the improvement of upland farmland from quarries at Penwyllt (SN 856 157). Christie declared bankruptcy in 1827, but his network of horse-drawn tramroads was pursued and extended by his creditors, eventually reaching a transhipment point on the Swansea Canal at Cribarth. The line of the tramway can be followed running near parallel with the A4067 north of Glyntawe, where it passes the main tramway depot at Cnewr (SN 8905 2205). Remains of bridges and some of the setts used to fix the iron plates to

The Cwm Prysor viaduct was opened in 1882 on the Bala-Ffestiniog branch of the Great Western Railway, a line that closed in 1961 when Llyn Celyn reservoir was constructed.

The Great Western & Rhymney Railway, Taf Bargoed branch, opened in 1876.
Part of the line remains in use for transporting coal from opencast mines,
while above Merthyr Tydfil the tracks have been taken up.

the ground can be seen in places. Running parallel to it is the line of the locomotive-worked railway that replaced it, The Neath & Brecon Railway which opened in 1867 and closed in 1962.

The railways that traversed the Welsh uplands fall into two main categories: narrow-gauge railways engineered primarily to carry freight (many of which have been preserved), and standard-gauge railways that were closed in the wake of the Beeching cuts of the 1960s. The Bala and Ffestiniog Railway was opened in 1882 from Bala to Trawsfynydd, where it traversed the high ground of Cwm Prysor. It was an important route at a time before the present A4212 was built in the 1960s. The line closed in 1961, when part of the line was flooded to create Llyn Celyn reservoir, but the line of it is well preserved on the hillside between Llyn Celyn and Trawsfynydd, and remains an impressive engineering achievement, with bridges over the descending streams, including the upper reaches of Afon Prysor.

4

MONUMENTS

PREHISTORIC

'LEAVE no trace' is the mantra of the modern outdoor movement, but, in the past, generations of people have set out to do precisely the opposite. The very earliest surviving archaeological remains in the uplands landscape are in the form of monuments; some of the most recent ones are too, even if they are very modest – think of the bench overlooking a grand view which was put there in memory of someone 'who loved this place'. There is a period of more than three millennia during which the archaeological record is dominated by monuments. These were created by people whose most tangible legacy is not the clearance of forests and the creation of farmsteads – as we might expect of the so-called Neolithic revolution when farming was first introduced – but the putting up of stones and the raising of mounds of earth or stone, altering the earth for non-practical reasons.

The chief legacy of Neolithic communities remains their chambered tombs, although only a minority of the surviving examples are found in the uplands and valleys. Even so, it is questionable whether the urge to build monuments was directly related to the adoption of farming techniques. Ironically, monument-building appears to have been the most prolific in the last areas of Europe where the Neolithic way of life was established – the Atlantic seaboard from Spain and Portugal to the Orkneys and eastwards, through southern Scandinavia, taking in Brittany, Britain and Ireland, and including the whole of Wales.

These are also areas where stone is abundant – timber constructions are far less durable over a long period of time. Even so, and based on the archaeological record, chambered tombs are far more common than their counterpart in eastern and southern England – the earthen long barrow.

Chambered tombs were built from about 4000–2300BC and were used for burying and commemorating the dead. The very idea of a chamber, which recreates the environment of a cave with its stone walls and a covering mound, suggests that these places are about a return to the Earth. Even so, only a handful of people could ever have been buried inside them, so for meaning we need to look beyond the role of burial chamber – perhaps to ancestor worship, placemaking, a sense of community in the past and present, and perhaps even staking a claim to territory. The use of monuments to lay claim to places could have been a serious matter to people who followed a semi-nomadic existence, driving livestock over the land according to the season, and who used the monuments for only part of the year. Excavations at the denuded chambered tomb at Gwernvale in the Black Mountains have

Arthur's Stone in the Gower is one of several chambered tombs
that overlook the coast of west Wales.

shown that the tomb, erected about 3500BC, was built on the site of a timber house that had been occupied for at least a century before the house of the dead superseded it. Even so, there is little evidence to show what people did when they gathered at such places.

Some chambered tombs are claimed to be related to specific places, even if the arguments occasionally sound a little tenuous. If you look at Pentre Ifan in Pembrokeshire (SN 0994 3701) from the right direction, its capstone mimics the profile of Carn Meini, the outcrop at the top of the Preseli Hills that is clearly visible from the monument. (This presupposes that the monument has never been restored and that the capstone is at the same angle it has always been.) Gwal y Filiast chambered tomb (SN 1705 2564) is a lowland monument in a wooded river valley in Carmarthenshire, its site said to have been influenced by the sound of the rushing Taf river. What is certainly uncontroversial is that many of the chambered tombs of south-west Wales overlook the coast, and it is difficult to argue that this was not significant.

Chambered tombs were typically constructed around a passage leading to multiple small chambers, or as a single chamber enclosed by large stones, or megaliths. The latter is the most common form in upland landscapes. Originally, they were partially covered by a surrounding mound of stones, either round or oblong in plan. The capstones are significantly larger than is needed simply to provide a roof over a chamber, and this suggests that they were meant to be seen and therefore protruded above the surrounding mound. In practice, the surrounding cairns are usually much denuded and can be difficult to identify, although if the outline can be traced it is sometimes possible to discern a formal entrance with forecourt and entrance façade. There are good, lowland, examples like Bryn Celli Ddu in Anglesey or Tinkinswood in the Vale of Glamorgan, that are restored sufficiently to show how these monuments once appeared. In the best examples there are multiple small chambers reached from a passage, all constructed of drystone walling. The foundations of Bedd yr Afanc (SN 1079 3459) chambered tomb in the Preseli Hills of Pembrokeshire is a good upland example. But on the high ground expect to find simpler

Maen-y-Bardd (Conwy) is typical of the chambered tombs in Wales, having a capstone far larger than is necessary simply to cover the chamber.

tombs comprising one large chamber defined by large uprights, or orthostats. In the most rewarding upland examples the megaliths have been left bare by the loss of the surrounding cairn, like Arthur's Stone (or Maen Ceti) in the Gower (SN 4913 9055), or survive with traces of a former long cairn, like Maen y Bardd (the Bard's Stone) above the Conwy Valley (SH 7406 7178).

Partial remains of chambered tombs of the Early Neolithic period are found across the uplands in Wales, but they are far outnumbered by the stone monuments of the later Neolithic and Early Bronze Age. The classic Bronze Age archaeological sites are stone circles, standing stones and cairns or barrows. Often all of these site types can be found in ritual complexes, sometimes also called ceremonial landscapes. Other types of monuments include henges, which are round enclosures defined by a bank and ditch rather than by stones. A henge is commonly associated with rivers and is therefore more often found in lowland landscapes (such as the Walton Basin in Radnorshire). Although the uplands have few of the most celebrated examples from this period, ceremonial landscapes are comparatively well-preserved

Maen Penddu (Conwy) may look like an isolated standing stone, but a careful search of the surrounding area will reveal related monuments, as well as a prehistoric route across the North Wales mountains.

here. In the lowlands, many of the ancillary stone monuments associated with stone circles and henges have disappeared as land use there has often been intensive. In the uplands, there has been much less pressure on land use. The moral, therefore, is that when you come across a Bronze Age monument, be on the lookout for others nearby. And remember that many landscapes from the Neolithic and Bronze Ages are buried by at least four millennia of accumulated soils, particularly in the case of those near coastal areas.

The stone circle has become the iconic form of Early Bronze Age monument, and has been exhaustively discussed. Were stone circles really solar observatories, as was once confidently asserted? The concept has gone in and out of fashion in archaeological debates, but it seems unlikely. The biggest problem of complex interpretations that rely on the exact positions of the stones is that the more intact a stone circle appears to be, the more likely it has been reconstructed at some point over the past two centuries. With unrestored circles, the stones have often fallen, and their exact position is uncertain. A stone circle is a ritual space, which we know because it is usually at the centre of a larger ritual landscape, with outlying stones and cairns that are clearly related to it. And the difference between stone circles and cairns may not be as great as first appears. There are examples in Wales that were once interpreted as stone circles, but are now understood to be the kerbs of now-vanished burial cairns, as explained below.

In Wales, the use of stones for circles and standing stones is similar to the pattern seen in south-west England, where the circles and rows are made up of stones from between ankle- and waist-height, as opposed to single standing stones, or pairs, which start at waist-height and often rise above head-height. The fact that none of the circles is as well known as the Cornish examples is simply because they are in remote and unvisited locations. There are no circles in Wales with the tall stones seen at places like Avebury, Callanish or Stenness.

The most famous stone circles in Britain (and stone circles are a very British thing) are found in accessible places like Wiltshire and west Cornwall where they have attracted attention for centuries, and the hand of restorers in the nineteenth and twentieth centuries is apparent and well-documented. The more remote upland stone circles of Wales were not discovered until archaeology became a discipline in the late nineteenth century, while the practical difficulty of finding them has been matched by the impracticality of restoring them. The advantage of this is that they have not been interfered with, but the disadvantage is that they are visually less impressive on first encounter. They may be a challenge to find, but the discovery is worth the hunt. At Nant Tarw, near the head of the River Usk in the Bannau Brycheiniog National Park, the stones of the two stone circles (SN 8187 2583) are small, barely 1m tall and many of them now mostly covered by turf. Cerrig Duon stone circle (SN 8513 2062), in the upper Tawe Valley, again in the Bannau Brycheiniog National Park, is also made up of small stones, mostly little more than half a metre tall, but it does have a taller outlying stone that makes it reasonably easy to find. These circles stand in moorland that looks barren from a distance, but discovering the stones changes our perception of the landscape as less inhospitable than it

The Druid's Circle above Penmaenmawr (Conwy) is close to the Graig Lwyd axe factories and stands amid a rich ceremonial landscape.

first appears. And bear in mind that the landscape environment four millennia ago may have been very different to that of today.

There are impressive stone circles that enclose open spaces, like the Druid's Circle (Maeni Hirion) above Penmaenmawr (SH 7228 7464) and Gors Fawr (SN 1346 2937) on the Preseli Hills. Gors Fawr is one of many stone circles that has taller outlying stones, and the circle itself is made up mostly of glacial erratics. Maen Penddu (SH 7390 7357), close to an important east–west route above the Conwy Valley, looks like an isolated standing stone but is in fact an outlier to the relatively inconspicuous Cefn Maen Amor stone circle (SH 7387 7359). The circle also has an outlying cairn. Cerrig Pryfaid (SH 7245 7132) is another circle that lies on an important route across the mountains of North Wales: a circle of ten stones that barely protrude above the surrounding grass. It stands in a landscape with two chambered tombs and abundant standing stones, perhaps acting as landscape markers that would have guided communities and their dead across the uplands.

The stone circle at Cerrig Duon (Powys) has a taller outlying stone known as Maen Mawr.

Gors Fawr stone circle in the Preseli Hills (Pembrokeshire) has outlying stones, one of which is visible in the background.

The pair of standing stones at Tafarn y Bwlch in the Preseli Hills are little above waist-height, unusual for standing stones in Wales.

Maen Llia (Powys) is one of the largest standing stones in Wales. It is unlikely to have been moved very far before it was raised upright.

Stone circles are the best-known form of stone setting that can be found in the Welsh uplands. There are also rows of stones, pairs and stones standing on their own. Stone rows are much rarer in Wales than on Dartmoor, but there is a fine example at Saith Maen (SN 8331 1540), above Glyntawe in the Swansea Valley. Lines of stones imply procession or at least directional travel, whether on foot or by eye. Solitary or pairs of standing stones are much more common and, because of their height, are much easier to identify. Some of them must be glacial erratics, which by their nature provide no evidence of their date and would have been very difficult to move from where they came to rest. Maen Llia (SN 9242 1918), near the head of Afon Llia in the Bannau Brycheiniog National Park, is so large it is hard to imagine that it was hauled, and still more difficult to imagine why it would be. It stands nearly 4m tall. The Preseli Hills' standing stones are also tall. Waun

A large stone-lined cist near Rowen (Conwy) is intermediate in scale between the Neolithic chambered tombs and Bronze Age cists.

Mawn standing stone is 2m high, whereas the nearby pair of stones at Tafarn-y-Bwlch are a bit less than shoulder-height. Some standing stones have been found to mark the position of burials, but most have not been excavated.

Cairns are the most common form of Bronze Age monument. Earthen barrows are very similar, but in Wales they are found mainly in the east, such as the Radnorshire hills, where stone is less plentiful on the surface. In most of Wales the presence of loose stones and the relatively thin soils made stone the obvious building material for burial mounds. Like the earlier chambered tombs, burials are covered by a round mound of stones but are enclosed in small stone-lined cists rather than large chambers, and wholly covered by the mound. These cists are a miniature version of the large single burial chambers found in the Neolithic uplands, and there are some examples where it is difficult to be certain whether they belong to the Neolithic or the Bronze Age, which began about 2300BC. Two examples of uncertain date are the Bailey Bach round cairn on the hills near Upper Chapel north of Brecon (SO 0304 3928), and a cairn at Rhiw (SH 7412 7188), close to the Neolithic Maen-y-Bardd chambered cairn above the Conwy Valley. Both have chambers that are enclosed by relatively large capstones supported by edge-set stones but are much smaller than the earlier Neolithic examples.

Cairns and barrows vary considerably in their size – between 5m and 50m in diameter – while they can be up to 5m tall. Cairns can be relatively sophisticated in their design and the form in

Stone slabs line the cist once buried beneath a cairn in the Rhinog mountains (Gwynedd).

Moel Ty Uchaf in the Berwyn Mountains near Llandrillo (Denbighshire), is a kerb cairn with a circular depression in the centre where the cist has been removed.

which we find them today may be the culmination of several phases of construction. The simplest form is the round heap of stones. Most summit cairns are of this type. Others are carefully structured, and the most common forms are ring cairns and kerb cairns.

It is easy to mistake a kerb cairn (also known as a cairn circle) for a stone circle and the difference between the two may not be as great as at first appears. The best example is probably Moel Ty Uchaf (SJ 0560 3717), near Llandrillo in the Berwyn Mountains, as impressive as any stone circle in Wales. It is a large circle of closely-set stones, in the centre of which is a clear circular depression which probably once contained a burial cist. Creigiau Eglwyseg cairn circle (SJ 2282 4513), also in the Berwyn Mountains near Llangollen, is another good example of a once very impressive, but unrestored, cairn circle. It is not a complete ring but retains 38 of its original stones, set with a bank around it; although most of them have been displaced and/or are lying flat on the ground, so it is difficult to imagine what it would originally have looked like.

A large kerb cairn on the slopes above Llyn Brenig (Denbighshire).

A large ring cairn at Cefn Sychbant (Powys), close to Llwyn-Onn reservoir, in a landscape of natural sink holes.

As their name suggests, ring cairns are formed of a ring of stones on the ground, which form a closed enclosure (they can be distinguished from hut circles, described below, because they usually cover areas too wide to be roofed and because there is no opening that marks a former entrance). Some of them are large. Of the two fine ring cairns at Cefn Sychbant, on the west side of Llwyn-Onn reservoir, the largest is over 20m in diameter (SN 9832 1087). The main burial would have been placed in the centre but there is no chance now of finding an intact cist.

In practice, most cairns have been denuded over the 4,000 years since they were constructed, partly by natural processes but mainly because of human intervention. Antiquaries of the nineteenth century were avid excavators of burials, often leaving no record of their activities. Archaeologists describe these people as grave-robbers, and the cairns as having been 'robbed out', although the perpetrators might well have described themselves as archaeologists. A pile of old stones is an easy quarry, and there are cairns that have been robbed for more mundane reasons – to create shelters for shepherds, drystone walls, sheepfolds or shooting butts in the nineteenth century. However, some have Ordnance Survey triangulation pillars on their summits, and there are practical reasons why many cairns have survived – many ridge-top cairns are significant landmarks that have subsequently been used as boundary markers.

The largest of the Brenig cairns (Denbighshire) was a ring cairn, later infilled to form a 'platform' cairn.

If cairns seem less impressive than chambered tombs, they compensate for it by their commanding positions in the landscape, and occasionally they exist in groups. There are summit cairns on many of the peaks of Welsh hills, but many of them are placed just off-centre enough to be more imposing when viewed from certain directions. There are also cairns placed on false crests so as to give a view of a surrounding landscape, very often in tight clusters or more scattered groups – but groups, nonetheless. The nature of hilly landscapes and their false peaks, as viewed from below, means that summit cairns often do not offer a view of the immediate surrounding landscape. Instead, the best view from the summit cairns is often of other summits with cairns.

One of the finest groups of Bronze Age cairns in upland Wales is found on the slopes above Llyn Brenig reservoir on the Denbighshire/Conwy border. These were excavated and restored in the 1970s in advance of the reservoir's construction, and constitute a fine example of an extensive ritual landscape. The restoration helps us to appreciate what these cairns must have looked like, and the impact they made on the landscape when they were completed. There is a large ring cairn (SH 9834 5720) at the water's edge that originally consisted of a ring of stones and an outer ring of wooden posts. Only later were cremated remains buried in the centre, followed by secondary burials. A nearby, simpler cairn (SH 9830 5726), known as Boncyn Arian, had a burial in the centre and others added later, but excavation revealed earlier phases, including circles of stakes and stones that were later covered with an earthen barrow. On the hillside above there is also a kerb cairn (SH 9953 5632), which might have been built over a prehistoric hut, but the principal interest is the large 'platform' cairn (SH 9898 5656). This began life as a massive ring cairn over 20m in diameter, the inner circle of which was marked by upright stones. When the site was excavated, cremation burials were found inside the ring and in the centre stood a wooden post. Later the open centre was infilled to create a large circular platform, and a small satellite cairn was added to the exterior in the form of a half circle.

Bryn Cader Faner (Gwynedd) is a cairn seemingly built over a ring of stone uprights.

Bryn Cader Faner (SH 6479 3529), below Moel Ysgyfarnogod in Merioneth, stands close to a Bronze Age route across Rhinog and is one of the more intriguing upland cairns. It has a ring of leaning, upright stones around the edge, as if it was a stone circle that was half-buried with a cairn. Most of the uprights are in their original positions, and others are lying horizontally. Where there is a hollow in the middle of the cairn, there was once a stone-lined cist, but this was removed sometime in the eighteenth or nineteenth century. The monument lies just below the summit of a rocky knoll and has a very striking appearance when it is viewed from the lower ground to the south-west. This was surely intentional and creates an unforgettable silhouette of a crown. One day, archaeological excavation may reveal whether the stone circle was an earlier monument over which the cairn was built.

The densest concentration of stone circles as the centrepieces of a ceremonial landscape is on the uplands above Penmaenmawr. It is not a coincidence that in the centuries around 3000BC this area was the third largest source of stone axes in the British Isles, and the track on the north side of the circle is considered to be of prehistoric origin, as already described. The main stone circle is known as the Druid's

Circle or Maeni Hirion, and unusually is surrounded by a bank, with a clearly defined entrance on the south-west side. When the site was excavated in the late 1950s a stone cist was found in the centre, along with evidence of cremation burials. The stone circle is on a plateau where there are numerous outlying monuments, including cairns and standing stones. Several rings of stones were probably mostly originally cairns, although there is a circle of five boulders which defies any of the categories that have been described here.

A similarly impressive ritual landscape can be found further east near Bwlch-y-Dduefaen, on the high plateau west of the Conwy Valley. The centrepiece was perhaps the stone circle (SH 7240 7130), where most of the stones have survived, albeit relatively inconspicuous now that they are partially grass-covered; but the numerous standing stones, which were described above, are unmissable, as is the earlier Maen-y-Bardd chambered tomb and a similar stone chamber set into the ground. What makes this ritual landscape especially interesting is that there is extensive evidence of settlement in later prehistory and the medieval period, while the route was later formalised as a Roman road.

A setting of boulders is one of numerous monuments in the ceremonial landscape above Penmaenmawr (Conwy).

EARLY-MEDIEVAL

Standing stones came back into fashion in the centuries following the end of the Roman occupation of Britain. A lot of these stones would be regarded as Bronze Age standing stones were it not for the inscriptions found on them, and there has always been a suspicion that they are prehistoric stones appropriated by a new generation. Traditionally these have been interpreted as grave markers, which in theory could be proved by a simple excavation. In practice, so many of these stones have been moved over time that their original context, which might have yielded evidence of burial, has been lost. Even some of the best-known examples that are still found in the landscape, like Maen Madoc (SN 9182 1577) beside Sarn Helen, have been re-erected in modern times and are not in their original position.

The earliest of these, and those found in the uplands, are the simple unworked stones. The tradition of finely-carved crosses, which continues into the Christian era and flourished until the eleventh century, is not found on the open moorland of Wales. Stones inscribed with a Latin or Ogham inscription are found across the landscape, of which

This early-medieval inscribed stone on Gelligaer Common (Glamorgan) once bore an inscription reading NEFROIHI, probably a reference to a local warlord.

Replica of the Cantiorix Stone beside Sarn Helen.

the Ogham stones are concentrated in south-west Wales. Ogham script comprises a series of straight cuts applied to the angles of upright stones. Although the most famous inscribed stones are now mainly found in churchyards, or even inside the church, there are some examples on the open hillsides. The only drawback to this is that they are likely to have succumbed to weathering more than their indoor counterparts. Maen Madoc still bears an inscription but it is now extremely difficult to make out. It reads 'DERVAC(VS) FILIUS IVST(US) (H) IC IACAIT' – 'here lies Dervacus, son of Justus'. The Ponsticill, or Cwm Criban, inscribed stone (SO 0726 1317), is only waist high, which makes it less likely that it could have been a prehistoric standing stone, and has an Ogham inscription that reads MAQI DECEDA, or 'son of Maqi'. The vulnerability to weathering that encouraged their removal by antiquaries to sheltered places, is well represented by the Cantiorix Stone in Penmachno Church, Eryri. It reads 'CANTIORI(X) HIC IACIT/ (V)ENEDOTIS CIVIE(S) FVIT (C)ONSOBRINO(S)/ MA(G)LI/ MAGISTRATI', 'Cantiorix lies here. He was a citizen of Venedos [i.e. Gwynedd] and cousin of Maglos the Magistrate', which is a particularly interesting and unusual inscription because it indicates the lingering influence of Roman culture. The stone stood by Sarn Helen near Llan Ffestiniog, where a replica was set up in 2006 (SH 7250 4267).

MODERN

Upright stones disappeared from the landscape in medieval times but commemorative stones, grave markers and some more ambitious architectural monuments have made a comeback in more modern times. Perhaps these constructions, which are variously about commemoration, status and territorial dominion, have more in common with ancient monuments than we might at first think.

Very few people will have seen the slate memorial stone to John Jones of Talsarn (SH 7200 5290), on the moorland above Dolwyddelan Castle. Set up after his death in 1857, it commemorates a sermon given by the Calvinistic Methodist minister at this spot in 1821. Much more familiar to hikers is the obelisk commemorating five-year-old Tommy Jones (SO 0005 2175), who died, lost and alone, near Corn Du in the Bannau Brycheiniog National Park in the summer of 1900. A roadside stone commemorates David Davies of Glynclawdd, who was killed at the limestone quarries in the Black Mountains in 1884 (SN 7315 1905). While most are made of stone, there are also cast-iron markers, like the curious memorial on Mynydd Farteg Fawr near Blaenavon commemorating Carlo, the setter belonging to Henry Kennard of Crumlin Hall, who accidently shot his favourite companion on 12 August 1864 (SO 2515 0679). The mid-nineteenth-century Tredegar Ironworks cholera cemetery (SO 1388 0758), and the more recent Jewish cemetery near Cefn-Coed-y-Cymmer (SO 0245 0884) are a different story. Both were established in open upland landscapes that seem to emphasise the outsider status that their occupants experienced in life. The Jewish cemetery served the significant Jewish population that gravitated to the iron industry in Merthyr Tydfil. This was established in 1865, but was expanded in 1935 to accommodate the Jewish community across a wider area.

A monument to a monument: a bluestone at Mynachlog Ddu in the Preseli Hills (Pembrokeshire) was set up in 1989 to commemorate the origin of the Stonehenge bluestones.

Not all monuments commemorate the dead. There are upland monuments that glorify the living and celebrate great events. The Jubilee Memorial Tower, on Moel Famau (SJ 1610 6266) in the Clwydian range, was an Egyptian-style tower designed by Thomas Harrison, built to commemorate the Golden Jubilee of George III in 1810. It fell during a storm in 1862, and now only the plinth remains. Its existence is a sign that the uplands were being visited by more than shepherds; but other monuments did not need to be viewed close-up. The Kymin near Monmouth may be more famous, but Admiral Rodney's Pillar (SJ 2951 1441), only just inside Wales on the Breiddin Hills, is just as good an example of the triumphalism of the Imperial era. It occupies a commanding position above the Severn Valley and is visible for miles around from both sides of the border. It was erected in 1781–2 to commemorate victory over the French fleet at Dominica in the West Indies, in ships that tradition says were constructed from Powysland oaks.

Admiral Rodney's Pillar on Breidden Hill (Powys) is a triumphalist monument commemorating victory over the French fleet in the West Indies. It was set up in 1781–2 overlooking the River Severn.

In the cemetery above Tredegar are the graves of cholera victims of the 1832 and 1849 epidemics, mostly people employed at the Tredegar Ironworks.

The base of the Jubilee Tower on Moel Famau (Flintshire/Denbighshire border)
gives some idea of the scale of the original monument built in 1810.
The rest of the structure fell in 1862.

Landowners also built their own monuments, a form of bizarre ostentation that has rarely stood the test of time and brings to mind Shelley's famous poem *Ozymandias* as a tangible demonstration of how all vanity is futile. The Crawshay family owned ironworks in Merthyr Tydfil and Hirwaun, and in the nineteenth century built a tower (SN 9411 0440) on the mountain between the two. Difficult to get to, and with no obvious purpose except to emphasise that the Crawshays once ruled over these hills, only the base of it survives. A similar fate befell the Biddulph Tower (SJ 1881 3910) near Glyn Ceiriog. It was erected by or for Robert Myddleton Biddulph (1805–72), owner of the Chirk Estate, but it is now little more than a pile of rubble. As if to rub it in, the rubble has been used to build up a small cairn, a little monument to the common rambler.

Part of the multivallate defences at Penycloddiau hillfort in the Clwydian Hills (Flintshire).

5

HILLFORTS AND HUT CIRCLES

ILLFORTS are the type of site most associated with the Iron Age, although many have their origins in the later Bronze Age. They are large enclosures, usually but not exclusively, on defensible high ground, and are among the biggest archaeological sites in the uplands, or indeed anywhere. They are usually described according to the number of banks and ditches that surround them – univallate, bivallate and multivallate for one, two and multiple; and their topographical position – promontory and contour hillforts. Hillforts were built, altered and inhabited over a long period of time, mainly from the first millennium BC until at least the Roman Conquest of Wales in AD 78. Some were re-occupied at a later date, such as Carn Fadryn (SH 2800 3520) on the Llŷn Peninsula, where the site was re-fortified in the medieval period.

Hillforts are not found in equal numbers in every region of Wales. There are comparatively few in the uplands of the South Wales valleys, for example, but otherwise they are a familiar sight and easy to spot. Even so, they are surprisingly little studied and very few of them have been subject to archaeological excavations, which in the past encouraged a tendency for sweeping generalisations in their interpretation. The few large hillforts that have been extensively excavated (not all in Wales) have influenced our general understanding of them, but they are not necessarily representative of hillforts as a whole. The most significant is Maiden Castle in Dorset, which was excavated by Sir Mortimer

Wheeler (formerly Director of the National Museum of Wales) in the 1930s and revealed clear evidence of a successful attack by the Roman army. As a result, the defensive function of these sites, and the threat of Roman attack, has been over-emphasised in our understanding of them. If they were defended against hostile forces, those enemies were likely to be closer to home, but evidence of actual armed conflict is generally missing from Welsh hillforts.

So what were they built for? There is no simple answer, largely because although they look similar they seem to have been built for a variety of reasons and were occupied over very long periods during which time societies are likely to have changed considerably. Archaeologists have therefore had to come up with a suite of interpretations to explain hillforts because if ever a single interpretation is put forward a large proportion of hillforts can be found that contradict it. The defensive capabilities of these sites was clearly a factor, although 'hillfort' has never been a very satisfactory term. So we have to bring in ideas about status, political power, social cohesion, settlement and farming if we are to make progress in understanding them.

Study hillforts closely and it soon becomes apparent that their defensive capabilities are variable, and sometimes were as much symbolic as practical. In most parts of Wales the defences are earthworks, although in Gwynedd there are hillforts with stone ramparts. Some of the grander hillforts have complex entrances. A good example is Pen-y-Bannau (SN 7419 6689) that overlooks Tregaron Bog in Ceredigion. It has an impressive and formidable-looking entrance, seen to its best advantage by people approaching from the mountains to the northeast. As a defensive site it was clearly more vulnerable from this higher ground, and the elaborate entrance may have given the impression of impregnability; but, as it was the main approach to the site for people coming in peace as well as war, it could just as easily have been designed to impress as a high-status site. The remainder of the hillfort is only very lightly defended, even though the banks may have carried a timber palisade – for people coming in peace or war, Tregaron bog would not be a good place to start.

The other picture conjured by the larger hillforts is that these were the equivalent of the modern village, but if you expect to find evidence of houses and other buildings you will usually be disappointed. Many of the smaller 'hillforts' were probably large defensible farmsteads, and the larger hillforts may have been larger examples of the same, serving a larger community or expressing the status of a more powerful individual. Evidence of settlement is usually found in the form of levelled ground, or platforms, on which roundhouses were built (described in more detail below). In the rockier hillforts of Gwynedd, evidence of hut circles and stone-walled enclosures is often clearly visible, as at Carn Fadryn and Tre'r ceiri (SH 3734 4467). In the Clwydian Hills, Penycloddiau hillfort (SJ 1290 6761) has a number of discernible levelled platforms that indicate that there were once numerous buildings within the ramparts. Standing on Foel Drygarn in the Preseli Hills (SN 1577 3360), where the interior is occupied by three earlier large Bronze Age cairns and where the high ground is steep and rocky, it is difficult to be convinced that you are in the forerunner of the modern idea of a village. But over 250 house sites have been identified within the enclosures, not all of them occupied at the same time – excavation in 1899 uncovered numerous Iron Age and Roman-period artefacts. Foel Drygarn also serves to remind us that, where hillforts enclose earlier archaeological features, they are likely to be funeral monuments rather than settlement evidence. There is no indication that the monument-builders of the Neolithic and Early Bronze Age built their homes on the hilltops, but what is especially interesting is that the cairns of Foel Drygarn were respected by later inhabitants and were not plundered as an easy quarry for building stone.

Like high-status buildings of any period, the position of hillforts in the landscape was important. When on a hillfort, you only need to look around you to understand why it is there. Hilltop sites are ideal for commanding territory, but some hillforts are carefully located in order to be seen, which may explain why some hillforts are set below hilltops in positions that, in theory, might make them vulnerable to attack from higher ground. Caer Drewyn (SJ 0876 4439), in the

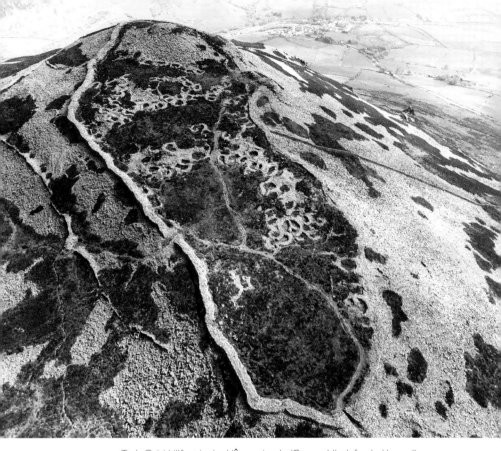

Tre'r Ceiri hillfort in the Llŷn peninsula (Gwynedd), defended by walls and with evidence of dense settlement inside it (*see detail overleaf*).

Berwyn Mountains near Corwen, seems an unlikely position for a hillfort, on the steep lower slopes of a prominent spur, but it overlooks the confluence of the Dee and Alwen rivers, which probably explains why it is there. As a sloping site the interior of the hillfort is clearly visible from below, which may be considered a weakness in military terms. Despite this, Caer Drewyn remained occupied for a long period, beginning with a small earthwork at the top of the hill, then later extended by means of a stone wall rather than the more common bank and ditch (probably utilising the natural scree material on the hillside). Traces of ancient fields on the hill above the fort are possibly contemporary with it.

To complicate matters further, not all hillforts were habitable enclosures, and therefore could only have been used on a temporary basis.

Pen-y-Gaer (SH 5865 4575) is described as a defended enclosure and is a good example of a 'hillfort' that is difficult to imagine ever being a settlement. It is situated below the pass of Bwlch Cwmystradllyn, which appears to have been an important route between the sea and Aberglaslyn in the heart of Eryri. The terrain here is uneven and very rocky, which would have made it particularly unsuitable for permanent habitation, or for impounding livestock, for which in any case there is no evidence. But it does guard an important route and commands a fine view westwards across to the coast near modern Porthmadog. In the valley below, there are numerous farmsteads and related small enclosures, and perhaps the defended enclosure provided protection or a special meeting place for these communities within a day's walk of the coast.

There are also smaller defended enclosures, sometimes called ring-works. Two important examples have been excavated, at Castle Odo (SH 1870 2846) and Meillionydd (SH 2188 2907), both on the Llŷn Peninsula. They have revealed early phases where the enclosure was defined by a timber fence, later strengthened by banks, and where occupation continued for several centuries; at first with timber round-houses and later with stone roundhouses. Other than being smaller, and therefore intended for a smaller, or perhaps more select, group of people, their purpose does not appear to have been different from the larger hillforts.

Tre'r Ceiri is one of the most spectacular of Welsh hillforts, on a steep and narrow hilltop site on the Llŷn Peninsula. Translated, it means 'Town of the Giants'. The site is a forbidding one, with its slopes covered in scree, but it certainly enjoys a commanding position. It is one of the best Welsh hillforts to visit because its component parts are well-preserved and are picked out in stone, making them easily visible and understood. In the middle of the hillfort is a much-earlier Bronze Age cairn on the summit of the hill. The hillfort is bounded by a single rampart, which is huge and stone-built, like many of the Gwynedd hillforts. On the north and west sides is a second wall, where the hillfort was most vulnerable to hostile forces, so it was certainly

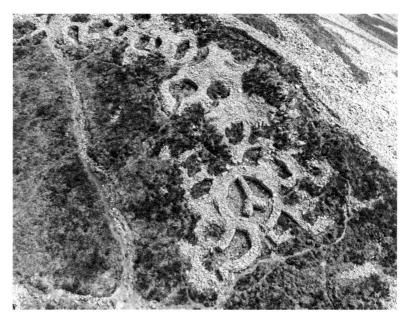
Hut circles inside Tr'e Ceiri hillfort.

defensible. The gateways have narrow, restrictive passages, which were designed so that an all-out attack would be difficult, although there were also minor gateways so that the inhabitants could leave the compound to fetch water or tend livestock. The defences date from the first century AD, but the site was evidently occupied much earlier. Despite its formidable and intimidating appearance, it has some of the best visible evidence of occupation found in the hillforts of Wales. Inside the rampart, structures that were once roundhouses are clearly discernible, together with some rectangular structures, and unroofed enclosures, which show that the place was inhabited until the fourth century AD if not later.

The Clwydian Range has a fine line of hillforts on or close to its ridges, which provide extensive views of land to the west over the Vale of Clwyd and in the direction of Eryri, north to the Irish Sea and east to the Cheshire Plain. But they are not a homogenous group. The two largest are Foel Fenlli, at nearly 10 hectares, and Penycloddiau, the largest hillfort in Wales, at nearly 19 hectares. The mainly bivallate

Foel Fenlli (SJ 1632 6008) is wrapped around a hilltop and overlooks the pass of Bwlch Penbarra, where there is now a minor road between Mold and Llanbedr Dyffryn Clwyd. Inside the hillfort are clear traces of settlement in the form of round platforms, where the ground was levelled for the building of houses. Penycloddiau (SJ 1290 6761) is multivallate, but also has similar evidence of settlement. Other sites are much smaller and may have been defended farmsteads, or the preserve of elite members of society. Moel Arthur (SJ 1453 6604) is a rounded univallate enclosure on a conical hilltop. The most intriguing is perhaps Moel y Gaer (SJ 1487 6175; not to be confused with the other nearby Moel y Gaer hillforts in Bodfari and Rhosesmor) because it does not occupy the highest ground and the entrance to it is on the uphill side, from where it would obviously be vulnerable to attack. Radiocarbon dating has suggested that it was built in the period 800–500BC and archaeologists have shown that when first built its ramparts were impressively stone-fronted. It has a commanding view over

Moel Arthur is a small and lightly defended hillfort on a conical peak in the Clwydian Hills (Flintshire).

Moel y Gaer (Flintshire) is usually referred to as a 'camp'. It is a simple enclosure where excavations in 1972 revealed substantial evidence of occupation.

the Vale of Clwyd to the west and evidence of settlement inside the enclosure in the form of levelled platforms. Each of these hillforts has produced evidence of occupation continuing into the Roman period. The most notable find is a hoard of over 1,500 Roman coins discovered at Foel Fenlli in 1816.

There exists other evidence of how and where people lived in the uplands in later prehistory, in contrast to the elusive evidence of settlement in earlier prehistory. First, it is worth mentioning the most abstruse of prehistoric secular monuments – the burnt mound. These are considered to be mostly of Bronze Age date and are another sign of prehistoric domestic life. They survive as circular or crescent-shaped mounds of fractured or burnt stone. They have been interpreted as cooking places or evidence that the equivalent of North American sweat lodges existed here. A burnt mound is difficult to identify on the ground, although many examples are labelled as such on Ordnance Survey maps. They are not photogenic and are usually overgrown.

A round hut on the pass above Llyn Cwmystradllyn (Gwynedd),
with the high mountains of Eryri in the background.

A round hut in Eryri with Yr Wyddfa in the background (Gwynedd).

The earliest form of domestic structure to be found on the Welsh hills is the roundhouse, often referred to as a hut circle. As a general rule, if the foundations of a stone building are rectangular, they are medieval or later; if round, they are earlier. Roundhouses can date from the Bronze Age to the Romano-British period and are, by their appearance alone, impossible to date more precisely. Roman period does not mean Roman-influenced, however, as these represent a long-standing native tradition.

Roundhouses had low walls and steep conical roofs covered with thatch. The low walls were usually built with field stones, and were round because it was easier than constructing a rectangular building with right angles. The low, stone walls kept the timber off the ground but also provided a flat base on which to build the roof; equivalent to the sills of medieval timber-framed buildings. An impression of how roundhouses originally appeared can be seen by visiting Castell Henllys Iron Age Village in Pembrokeshire, where such buildings have been reconstructed.

The position of later Bronze Age and Iron Age dwellings may still be identified, even where there are no longer any stone footings in evidence or they originally had timber or clay walls (generally earlier in date than the stone roundhouses). For practical reasons habitations were built on level ground, which, on sloping hillsides, meant levelling the ground artificially before construction began. The levelled ground is known as a platform, examples of which from hillforts have been described above. Are they easy to spot? Not to the unpractised eye, but hillfort interiors are a rewarding place to start looking for them because you will know that evidence of domestic life is expected there.

Most hut circles are not found in hillforts but either individually or in groups on the open hillside, generally favouring sheltered positions. Hut circles are more common in the stonier parts of the Welsh uplands, which means the north-west and the uplands of the Bannau Brycheiniog National Park. The higher the ground, the smaller the roundhouse is likely to be. Individual roundhouses on higher ground may have been summer dwellings only, a pattern of seasonal grazing to which we will return in later centuries. Where they are set in an enclosure, they have the character of a simple farmstead in which the livestock are penned rather than grazing in an open landscape. This,

An Iron Age round hut with a square annex, close to Sarn Helen near Llan Ffestiniog (Gwynedd).

however, takes us beyond the Iron Age, from whence there is more settlement evidence. The latest of the hut circles very often have a rectangular annexe or a detached rectangular structure. These structures are probably later in date and belong to the Romano-British period and were perhaps animal houses or had other specialised purposes. Although the enclosures were probably mainly for grazing livestock, in some cases they have been cleared of stones and exist as terraces, which might also have allowed crops to be planted there.

North-west Wales has a rich heritage of small farmsteads of the Iron Age and Roman periods, some of which are enclosed by banks and ditches (nominally defended settlements), while others have traces of small fields, which existed in an otherwise unenclosed landscape. This has been termed an infield-outfield system of agriculture, in which the outfield is represented by the extensive pasture of the open hills. It is a pattern of settlement that is recognisable in recent centuries, but from

Maes y Caerau (Gwynedd) is a single round hut enclosed by two concentric walls, a small defended homestead. Nearby (not shown in the picture) are areas of cultivation ridges that are probably contemporary.

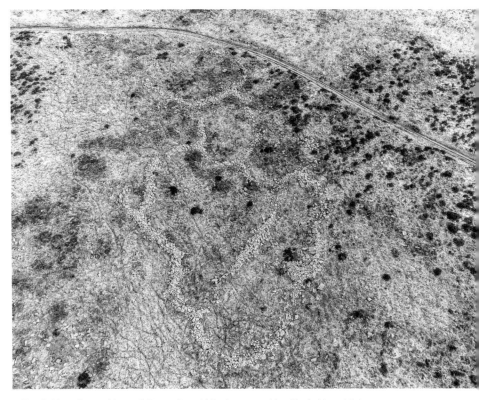

The fields and round huts of Carreg Lwyd (also known as Hen Dre'r Mynydd) form a substantial Iron Age settlement above Blaenrhondda (Rhondda Cynon Taf).

the medieval period changes in settlement patterns start to become apparent (if only because we have historical sources that give some indication of upland life) and the extent of outfield effectively began to shrink.

Open settlements comprising groups of hut circles, perhaps with associated field systems, are found in the uplands of South Wales and have been interpreted as an alternative to the hillforts found elsewhere. High and conspicuous positions seem not to have been key to their locations, and the well-preserved examples at the head of the Rhondda Valley and on Hirwaun Common may be upland examples of a common settlement type that was once found in the lowlands too. Carreg Lwyd (SN 923 019), on the hill above Blaenrhondda, is made up

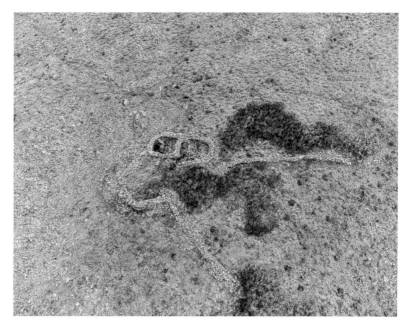

At the Iron Age settlement at Mynydd Cefn y Gryngon on Hirwaun Common (Rhondda Cynon Taf) the structures were partially adapted to create a post-medieval sheepfold.

of several round and sub-rectangular structures. The settlement found on Hirwaun Common at Mynydd Cefn-y-Gyngon (SN 9573 0340) is similar, where longevity of use is evidenced by the later construction of rectangular structures, and by the adaptation of one of the hut circles to create a sheepfold.

6

Homesteads and farmsteads

Evidence for dwellings is much more numerous for medieval and later centuries. However, one of the important themes of upland archaeology is continuity, although the concept is often very difficult to appreciate when encountering the remains of a former house in the uplands. But everyday life did not change dramatically after the Romans left, and the places that suited settlement in the Iron Age remained prime sites for settlement in later periods. Occasionally this evidence is obvious, as in Mynydd Cefn-y-Gyngon between Hirwaun and Aberdare (SN 9573 0340), described in the previous chapter. It also applies to hillforts and some Roman forts that were re-occupied in the historic centuries.

There are several early upland Welsh defended sites which had previously been the site of Iron Age hillforts (there was not necessarily a continuity of occupation), but they did not always house royal courts and were not always built with a view to repelling hostile visitors. A good example of re-use is the Iron Age hillfort Castell Caerau above Dolbenmaen on the Llŷn Peninsula (SH 5090 4392). But this appears to have been secondary to the motte on lower ground in Dolbenmaen, and may have been occupied as a military site as a pair with another similar site on the opposite side of the Dwyfor at Craig y Tyddyn (SH 5055 4275).

There are remains of elite dwellings in the uplands, dating almost entirely from the medieval period. Although they are often discussed as defensive sites, they were invariably more residential than military.

Relatively few of these are now found on open moorland, but there are many examples on high ground, like Cymer Castle near Dolgellau or Carreg Cennen near Llandeilo, that are now within a landscape of fields.

The earliest form is the motte, or castle mound, on which a timber keep was built. This is a type of fortification built across Europe, with a few native-built examples in Wales, which were raised in the eleventh and twelfth centuries and are roughly contemporary with those built in England. Perhaps the best upland example in Wales is at Tomen-y-Mur (SH 7054 3868), built on the site of a Roman fort. Tomen-y-Mur is in a strong position with extensive views, including to the coast at Trawsfynydd. This strategic importance was amplified by the construction of the Roman road network that linked its fortifications. This road network is likely to have been functioning in the early medieval period at least. The earlier earthworks effectively acted as a bailey for the mound, on which a timber keep was built (*Tomen-y-Mur* means 'mound on the wall'). Who built it is less obvious. It has been attributed to William Rufus (William II of England, who reigned from 1087 to 1100), who was campaigning in this area in 1095. But it looks more like a permanent defendable residence and therefore was probably a royal court of the Princes of Gwynedd. This is how it is described in *The Mabinogion*, where it is referred to as Castell y Mur. Like many such mottes it was later superseded by a house on level ground, although in this case it was a mere farmhouse (SH 7061 3872).

Castell y Mur was an important site but upland high-status houses of the early-medieval period are actually very rare. The Anglo-Norman invaders preferred strategic riverside locations for their castles, such as Chepstow, Cardiff, Swansea, Kidwelly, Pembroke and so on, while the castles of Edward I were riverside and/or coastal sites, like Caernarfon, Conwy, Harlech, Rhuddlan and Aberystwyth. It is the Welsh castles that are usually found in upland regions, or commanding high positions. Dolforwyn Castle was built in a commanding position over the Severn Valley by Llywelyn ap Gruffudd following the Treaty of Montgomery in 1267. It so irked the neighbouring Marcher lords – fearing a loss of their status as a bastion against a hostile Wales – that they persuaded

The restored remains of Tomen-y-Mur farmstead (Gwynedd), a post-medieval farm that superseded the motte on the site, which in turn superseded the Roman fort.

Edward I that Llywelyn's castle was a threat, the ultimate response to which was the invasion of North Wales in 1277. The subsequent fate of Dolforwyn, and the civilian settlement that had grown up around it, sums up the declining strategic importance of high ground. The English took, then abandoned, Dolforwyn, and replaced it with a new riverside settlement – Newtown by the River Severn.

In the uplands it is easier to build in stone rather than timber, and most of the surviving elite homes were stone-built. There are fragmentary remains of a small cluster of early stone-built castles in northwest Wales at Dinas Emrys (SH 6067 4922, by tradition the home of Vortigern and where the young Merlin made prophecies), Castell Pen-y-Garn (SH 5814 4119) and Carn Fadryn (SH 2800 3520). The latter, on the Llŷn Peninsula, was described as new by Gerald of Wales in 1188. Here, a castle was built on the highest point of a former Iron Age hillfort – no need to build a motte here.

Castle-building in stone continued into the thirteenth century. The best-preserved castle in an upland setting is perhaps Dolwyddelan (SH 7218 5234). It was preceded by a castle nearby at Tomen y Castell, one of the cluster of twelfth-century castles mentioned above, where Llywelyn the Great was probably born *c.*1173. It stands close to Afon Lledr but, interestingly, the castle that superseded it in the early thirteenth century was built by Llywelyn himself on much higher ground. Dolwyddelan was captured during Edward I's invasion of 1282–3 but, despite some alterations to the buildings, by the fourteenth century it had been abandoned. When it was leased again in the fifteenth century it was no longer a defensive stronghold, just a house.

Castell Dinas Bran overlooks the Dee Valley near Llangollen (SJ 2224 4306). Best-known now as a romantic hilltop ruin, it was built in stone in the second half of the thirteenth century, possibly by Gruffydd ap Madoc, son of the founder of Valle Crucis Abbey, but is surrounded by the earthwork enclosure of an Iron Age hillfort. After the conquest of Edward I it was abandoned in favour of a new castle at Holt by the River Dee – another case of forsaking the hilltop in favour of the

Castell Dinas Bran (Denbighshire), overlooking the Dee valley near Llangollen, was built in the thirteenth century on the site of an Iron Age hillfort.

Dolwyddelan Castle (Conwy) was built by Llywelyn the Great in the early thirteenth century: one of the last upland houses of elite status.

river bank. In South Wales, Carreg Cennen Castle (SN 6679 1907), overlooking the Cennen Valley, was probably built by John Giffard, first Baron Giffard – granted to him by Edward I after his conquest of Wales in 1283, although the family subsequently lost control of it and it eventually passed to the Crown. Owain Glyndŵr took it in 1403 and it was slighted in 1462 during the Wars of the Roses, one of the last hilltop strongholds to have seen armed conflict.

Thereafter the uplands provided homes only for the humbler classes of society. Remains of homes in the common era represent both permanent and seasonal dwellings, farmsteads with ancillary buildings and enclosures, isolated cottages and rows of industrial housing. The farmstead is obviously the most common type of home to be found in the upland archaeological record, but is variable in its scale and the complexity of its buildings. There is a traditional distinction in rural Wales between the home farm in the lowlands (*hendre*) and the more

An isolated house and enclosure, with no road or footpath now leading to it, at Ceunant Coch below Arenig Fawr (Gwynedd), was probably a *hafoty*, long-since abandoned.

rudimentary seasonal home in the uplands (*hafoty*), built within the summer pasture, or *hafod*. Seasonal dwellings in mid Wales are often known by the alternative name *lluest*. As far as we know, the distinction between winter and summer dwellings has its origin in the medieval period.

If you come across a house at high altitude it is likely to have been the house of a summer station, the *hafoty* (plural *hafotai*) or *lluest* but the history of these places is often more complicated. A house may have been built for summer use but later became a permanent farmstead (hence the common *hafod* place-name), or may have been a permanent farmstead that was retained only for seasonal use following a period of retreat from the marginal high ground. The majority of hafod place-names refer now to farms below the mountain land. But most of these seasonal dwellings were originally very rudimentary, even though they were intended for multiple occupation by a family, as distinct from the even simpler shepherds' huts. For example, John Leland, travelling through Ceredigion in the 1530s, noticed some 'very poor cottages for summer dairies for cattle'.

Many summer dwellings became permanent farmsteads, documenting the advance of settled farming on the high ground. Land in Beddgelert parish was mostly in the ownership of Aberconwy Abbey until the mid-sixteenth century and three of the hafod sites recorded in the sixteenth century can still be identified: Hafod-y-llan and Hafod-y-Porth are still farms but they are no longer sited in unenclosed uplands. Another, the ruined Hafod Wydir (SH 5767 5014) is on the fringe of the unenclosed uplands, but with its own story of relict medieval fields. On the remote Aberystwyth mountain road is Aber Glanhirin farmstead, an island amid the open moorland on the bank of the river above the Elan Valley reservoirs. The buildings are modern, and only the farm's remote location hints at its long history. It was established as a *lluest*, and was sold in 1585, probably marking its transition from seasonal use to a permanent farmstead. The sale in 1585 provided for enclosing about 80 acres of common land around the summer house.

Upper Cwm yr Ingel in Radnorshire (Powys) is a cruck-framed former farmhouse now relegated to farm use as the number of permanent farmsteads in the uplands has decreased.

Not all of these *hafotai* were built at a long distance from the main farmhouse. At Ty Nant (SH 9054 2623) in Cwm Cynllwyd, Llanuwchllyn, the former *hafoty* stands in a field only 450m from the farmhouse. At Maes y Gamfa near Dinas Mawddwy the *hafoty* (SH 8139 1356) is only 1.6km away, beyond Ffridd Maes y Gamfa, and built of mortared stone, suggesting a date no earlier than the eighteenth century. These are examples where the upland sheepwalk was on unenclosed land adjacent to the farm, but that was not always the case. In 1585 the summer house at Lluest Pen-y-Rhiw (SN 9309 7147) was sold with one of the farms at Nannerth, in the Wye Valley above Rhayader. Despite being only a mile apart, the two houses were in completely different landscapes, separated by a precipitously-steep valley side. In other cases the upland pasture was at a considerable distance. Lluest Aberceithon (SN 8749 6882), above Craig Goch reservoir in the Elan Valley, was first recorded in 1585 and has a ruined house dated 1815, but it is over 5 miles from Aberceithon as the crow flies, and a long way by road down the winding valley.

Apart from the minority of summer dwellings that became permanent farmsteads, many of these buildings were put to a variety of uses after the practice of seasonal movement had ceased; for example, by shepherds or during the sheep-shearing season. The principle reason for the decline of the summer dwelling was the decline in importance of upland pasture for dairy animals, including sheep, which is described in more detail in the chapter on farming.

Poor people were forced on to the unenclosed uplands in times of population growth and then deserted them when there were better opportunities elsewhere. There was depopulation from the uplands after the Black Death of the mid-fourteenth century, perhaps after the Glyndŵr revolt of the early fifteenth century, and in parts of Wales during the industrial revolution of the eighteenth and nineteenth centuries. From the late-seventeenth to the nineteenth centuries, the uplands and commons were colonised by the landless poor, creating what would now be regarded as smallholdings on previously unenclosed ground. Most of these in eastern Wales were on the edges of

Lluest Pen Rhiw (Powys), above the Wye Valley near Rhayader, was a *lluest* that later became a permanent farmstead, now long-abandoned

the commons, and, by enclosing ground around them, it has had the long-term unintended consequence of excluding this land from open access. Others remain as islands in the open moorland, or as abandoned farmsteads. Technically, many of these houses were illegal but enforcement in the remote rural parts of Wales was lax. The tradition has it that if a house was erected in one night and smoke was seen rising from its chimney by daybreak, then the right to settle there was established. These houses were known as a *ty unnos*, although in practice there was nobody around to check how long they took to build. These types of farmsteads began as a cottage surrounded by a small enclosure, then expanded with further enclosures as the smallholding became established. In the long run, many of these squatter settlements became legitimised when landlords turned things to their advantage by charging rent.

There is a lot of evidence of permanent farmsteads that were created on common land in Radnorshire, encroachments made as the uplands were repopulated after the decline of the fourteenth century. The historic Ordnance Survey maps mark many of them. Many of these encroachments, also known as squatter settlements, had ironic names, such as Paradise and Moelfre City (SO 115 756). The latter is a good example of farmsteads being established in more-or-less the same place as abandoned medieval farmsteads.

In 1744, Lewis Morris undertook a survey of a large tract of moorland, roughly 32,000 acres on the west side of Plynlimon, ostensibly as part of a mineral survey, but which now provides some quite detailed information on small upland farmsteads. At that time there were:

> [61] small cottages which were originally summer houses for shepherds and have an inclosure of a few acres of ground annexed to them. Most of them are habitable all the year round, paying rent to the owners generally under 20 shillings ... These cottages are called by the natives Lluestiau to distinguish them from the freeholds.

Eight of them were already in ruins but most continued to be occupied into the nineteenth century. Maesnant and Nant y Moch (with nearby chapel) were lost in the 1950s to the building of Nant y Moch reservoir, but evidence of many of these 'summer houses turned permanent farmsteads' can be found in the uplands on the west and north sides of Plynlimon Fawr, upstream of the reservoir, where there is a landscape of scattered tiny farmsteads in the unenclosed moorland. All had stone-built houses. The highest of them are above the 400m contour, such as Lluest y Meinciau (SN 7768 8760), in ruins by 1744 and where only traces survive, and Lluest Newydd (SN 7965 8951). Lluest Newydd survives as a ruined house, which was probably built in the eighteenth or early-nineteenth century. It is stone-built, consisting of two rooms on the ground floor and perhaps containing a sleeping area in the roof space. Attached to it is another unit, probably for farm use and housing cattle. Less than 200m away is the former Hengwm Annedd (SN 7974 8931), which was probably the house known as Lluest Fach Hengwm in the 1744 survey. Situated on the bank of Afon Hengwm, the ruins of this house are later, however, as the remains of the walls are high enough to suggest a two-storey house with two rooms in each storey and with a farm building attached. Further downstream to the west are the remains of Nant-y-Llyn (SN 7828 8902), which was another single-storey house with a fireplace, and probably of a similar date to Lluest Newydd. Further west is the remains of Llechwedd Mawr (SN 7619 8896), an upland farm just above the limit of Nant y Moch reservoir. As a permanent farmstead of at least eighteenth-century origin, it is a reminder that these now deserted moorlands could be seen as viable agricultural land. Llechwedd Mawr possessed nearly 900 acres of sheepwalks, as well as enclosed land nearer the farmhouse where cattle could be pastured. Perhaps against the odds, the farmhouse remains standing, although now given over only to farm use.

Lluest Newydd (Powys), probably built in the eighteenth century, is one of many ruined *lluestiau* on the moors above Nant y Moch reservoir.

Nant-y-Llyn (Powys) above Nant-y-Moch reservoir. The site of
the Battle of Hyddgen is on the distant moorland.

The elongated footprint of Hen Ddinbych (Denbighshire) stands within a
large embanked enclosure. Hen Ddynbich was a medieval monastic grange
that belonged to Denbigh Priory.

Although there are no houses of medieval date standing in open moorland today – the earliest of them can be dated to the sixteenth century – many remains of houses and farmsteads in the hills must have been associated with seasonal movement. According to Gerald of Wales, writing at the end of the twelfth century, the Welsh lived in wattled huts, put up with little labour or expense, which had a short lifespan of a year or two. While we do not want to give too much weight to a passing reference, there is some evidence to back up the general spirit of what Gerald was describing. A lot of the evidence for medieval houses survives in the form of earthworks, as described below. Medieval timber-framed buildings were set up with the base timber, or sill beam, directly on the ground. The lower timbers would rot over time, so, if a house was abandoned and its good timbers were either re-used or burnt as firewood, there would be little trace left. By contrast, where a house with either stone walls or stone footings was abandoned, it is unlikely that all of the stones would be removed from the site, except to put up a new building. Later on, it was standard practice to build a timber frame on a stone footing or sill. Likewise, houses which had earthen walls, common in parts of south-west Wales, were also built on stone sills. So the earthwork remains of houses are likely to have been timber-framed, whereas remnants of stone walls could indicate stone, timber-framed or earth-built houses. Timber was always needed for the roofs because stone-slab roofs can cover only a small span; but in parts of Wales where stone was easily available on the ground and where timber was in short supply, for example on higher ground, stone walls may always have been the norm.

Earthwork remains of houses are discovered in the form of building platforms, which are commonly found in the uplands and are especially abundant in parts of South Wales and in Powys, and are essentially levelled areas of ground on which a building was put up. The usual position is at the foot of a slope, where the ground could be dug out in order to lay the sill of the timber frame on level ground. The convention was to site the building with the narrow end facing the slope, because this is the optimum angle to reduce the effect of water running off the hill. This aspect, setting at right angles to the slope, remained the most common (but not universal) siting of houses in Wales until the nineteenth century.

Building platforms survive individually and in groups. Not every platform represents a house. Where there is a pair, it is likely that one is a house and the other is a cow house and the space between them was a farmyard. In other cases, where a platform seems very long for a house, it is most likely the remains of a house and a cow house attached in-line. The farmhouse with adjoining cow house in line was the most common arrangement in Welsh farmsteads as late as the nineteenth century.

The problem of rotting timbers in timber-framed buildings was alleviated by raising the sill on stone footings, acting as a damp course and providing a level base on which to construct the building. The stone footings of timber-framed buildings, and of ruined stone-walled buildings, are very common in upland landscapes. They are known as long huts by archaeologists, which is not a very inspiring name for one of the most commonly encountered features in the moorland land-scapes, but is a useful unspecific term. Long huts are found in surprisingly large numbers all over Wales, but are much more common in the stonier parts, for obvious reasons. Even so, there is no evidence that distinguishes the remains of a stone building from a timber-framed building on a stone base. The shape of them is also variable. The more rudimentary structures have rounded ends (a good sign that it was a stone building, as timber-framed buildings have square ends), although sometimes masonry falls in such a way that it is difficult to establish the original shape of a building's plan.

The phrase 'long hut' has been adopted merely because it describes the shape of a structure and not its use. Most would have been hab-itations of some sort, while others were animal houses. There is very rarely any evidence by which a structure can be dated, except by associa-tion with other features in the landscape. For example, where long huts are found in isolated positions away from an identifiable track they are likely to be early, although it does not follow that long huts by existing tracks are necessarily later. Evidence that a long hut might have been a

A building platform on the high ground above the Glaslyn valley in Eryri (Gwynedd).

Long huts are one of the most familiar sights on the hills and, apart from a date between medieval and the nineteenth century, their specific purpose is usually undetermined.

house include whether it has been built on a levelled platform, whether it is built with its end wall facing the slope, and whether there are associated field walls that show it was a farmstead. Presence of a fireplace will clinch it, except that most long huts will not have a fireplace. Integral fireplaces appeared in farmhouses in Wales from the sixteenth century but they tended to filter down from high to low-status homes, and so where fireplaces occur in poor upland cottages they could have been built as late as the eighteenth or nineteenth century.

There are groups of long huts that were occupied over a long period of time, although precise dates are elusive. There are, for example, two deserted small settlements near the head of Afon Cynfal (SH 7516 4131 and SH 7526 4083), above Llan Ffestiniog. Each has numerous long huts, some of them subdivided into two interior units, but some of the buildings overlie others and the latest phase of use was for penning sheep. The Iron Age settlement on Hirwaun Common has already been mentioned as a place re-occupied later, but there are rudimentary settlements here too that probably straddle the medieval

Hengae (Powys) was an isolated cottage, perhaps latterly used by a shepherd, beside the Monk's Trod in mid Wales. It was roofless by 1905 and now little more than the footprint of the cottage survives.

A long hut above the pass at Bwlch Oerddrws (Gwynedd) was perhaps used by the bandits said to lurk on the hills waiting for vulnerable travellers to pass by.

and post-medieval periods, like Mynydd Cefn-y-Gyngon and Tarren-y-Bwlch (SN 9511 0351), in a position overlooking the common but sheltered from the prevailing westerly winds.

Isolated long huts reveal little of their original intended domestic uses. For example, they might have been cottages built by poor people as permanent homes, or they may have belonged to a lowland farm and were used only seasonally. In landscapes with associated features it is also reasonable to speculate their provenance: that huts were built by fishermen if found by a lake; by gamekeepers if in a landscape of shooting stands; or by shepherds when in a high and otherwise inhospitable location.

The process of understanding upland life is made much easier when buildings are standing to their full height – it makes the interpretation of date and function so much easier. Farmhouses and cottages (*bwythyn*, defined as a home with insufficient land to provide a living) in upland landscapes have long been the kind of dwelling most vulnerable to rural depopulation, but they take a long time to fall down if left to their own devices. So it is not uncommon to find remains of houses where the walls stand high enough to distinguish doorways and windows, or even retain all or part of their roofs. The latter, of course, are often retained for farm use and are managed accordingly. And from a distance, old dwellings can be identified by the presence of one or more trees. These are common at post-medieval farmsteads or cottages, and were planted as windbreaks, providing some shelter on exposed hillsides.

There are some simple clues as to the date of these buildings. Local building materials were invariably used until well into the nineteenth century, at least for the walls, so a house built of brick is likely to be of relatively late date. In many parts of Wales, houses were of a single storey, perhaps with a sleeping space in the attic, known as a *croglofft* in North Wales, also until well into the nineteenth century. Two-storey houses tend to date from the second half of the nineteenth century, although there are, of course, exceptions. Other common signs of late date include a symmetrical arrangement of the windows in relation to the doors (earlier houses were asymmetrical because there was always one main room and a smaller one on the ground floor), and two chimney stacks rather than one.

Attached to and in line with the farmhouse there may be a cow house, known variously as a byre or, especially in north-east Wales, a *shippon*. This arrangement of house and cow house produces a long range which is often mistakenly referred to as a 'longhouse'. In practice, surviving true longhouses are very rare. A longhouse is not just a house that is long, but refers to a specific relationship between house and cow house. In a longhouse livestock and humans enter by the same door, then turn their different ways into their separate accommodation. In Wales, most farmsteads where the house and cow house are in line have separate entrances for people and animals.

Other buildings that could be found at farmsteads are very rare before the eighteenth century and are mostly of the nineteenth century. They include implement stores, often with external steps to a granary above, and a barn for storage and threshing. A common feature of north-west Wales is to have a small mill as part of the farmstead. These small mills on farms were invariably water-powered. Water was

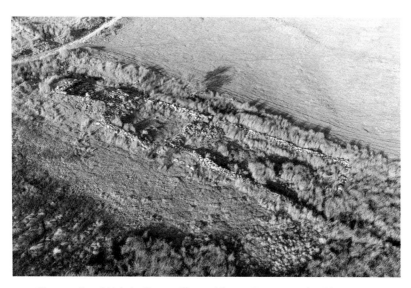

The remains of Hafod y Garreg (Gwynedd), a rudimentary upland farmstead, comprise the house (upper left), together with small enclosures or paddocks.

both a cheap and reliable source of power, although it required regular maintenance to keep the water channels clear. Mill buildings themselves can be difficult to identify. The tell-tale features are the presence of a linear pit on the side of the building – the wheelpit – and an axle or gear shaft, by which means power was transmitted to millstones. The water supply demanded careful management, even for a small mill that worked only intermittently, and so on the uphill side expect to find a small pond and a former watercourse that led to the wheel. Many of these were raised above ground in order that the water

The remains of the small farmstead wheelpit at Amnodd Wen, below Arenig Fawr (Gwynedd), are still visible, as are parts of the gearing that drove the millstones.

could be delivered to the top of the waterwheel, which leaves comparatively little trace except possibly for the stone or brick piers that carried the wooden trough. Wheelpits also have an outflow at the downhill end, so there may be the remains of another channel, known as the tail race, that delivered water back into a stream. As these were very small mills they were not normally of more than one storey, but there will be a window at least. The lack of a chimney distinguishes these small buildings from cottages.

Tai Cochion (sh 5815 4328) was a smallholding above the Glaslyn Valley south of Beddgelert, which amounted to only 15 acres in the mid-nineteenth century, with rights to hill pasture. It has a small, ruinous cow house and another farm building close to the house. A small mill was added to the house by the end of the nineteenth century. It was used to grind oats and perhaps rye too, grown in small stone-free strips on the hillside, but in quantities too small to justify

Tai Cochion is a small farmstead in Eryri (Gwynedd). The small range on the left is a nineteenth-century mill, the water from which drained via the tail race in the foreground.

the long and difficult journey to the nearest corn mill. Tai Cochion is unusual in preserving an identifiable mill and mill race, and also has a mill pond above the farmstead.

Although houses are not a common sight on the unenclosed uplands, the survival of groups of buildings can be evidence of once-important routes across the hills. An example is the string of former farmsteads and cottages between Llandecwyn and Trawsfynydd, across the mountainous terrain that shuts the coastline north and south of Harlech off from the rest of the mainland. Along the former road are surviving and ruined houses. The highest of them is Nant Pasgan Mawr (SH 6542 3656). It is a cruck-framed house with stone walls and probably always had two storeys – and therefore a substantial house. It has been dated by dendrochronology to the mid-sixteenth century. It always had a fireplace, next to which were the stairs. The profile of the building, with its steep roof pitch, is an indicator of its early date, but its length is evidence of additions made later. About 250m to the south-west is Nant Pasgan Bach (SH 6521 3636), which is a two-storey

Nant Pasgan Mawr in the Rhinogydd hills (Gwynedd), with its steep roof slope,
is one of the oldest surviving houses in the uplands of Wales.

house dated 1840. It was part of a much older farmstead, the ruins of which can be seen at a distance on the south side. In the space of less than one kilometre are other ruined farmsteads and cottages. Hendre Cerrig (SH 6474 3650) is a two-storey house with a cow house alongside, which was abandoned in the first half of the twentieth century and has been roofless ever since. Tal-y-Rhos (SH 6487 3642) is an eighteenth-century cottage, or 'tyddyn', that incorporates a house and byre in a single structure, with external steps to the accommodation in the attic storey, where there is a fireplace in the end wall. It was abandoned at the end of the nineteenth century and has been roofless for over a hundred years. Panwr (SH 6558 3655) is marked on the early Ordnance Survey maps as a house, although it is now a roofed structure without any obvious diagnostic features.

Expansion of mining and quarrying from the eighteenth century brought with it the need to accommodate workmen in remote locations. A place to live was often an essential incentive in acquiring a workforce. Industrial houses were built in the rural tradition, except

Nant Pasgan Bach (Gwynedd) is a house of two full storeys, which did not become common on the uplands until the nineteenth century.

This row of cottages, essentially traditional rural cottages joined in a line, was built for miners at Drws y Coed copper mine near Nantlle (Gwynedd).

that they are often joined together to create small terraces. In South Wales the early terraces associated with ironstone mining and iron smelting have either been pulled down or have been enveloped by larger and later settlements. North Wales has the best remaining examples in the remote hills, mainly for those working in the slate industry, but also houses associated with metal mining.

A village might seem like a contradiction in terms when thinking about upland landscapes, but they existed and can be found, particularly associated with the slate industry. (It is also worth remembering that the town of Blaenau Ffestiniog was built in a remote upland landscape and remains a functioning town.) Treforys was built in the 1850s for quarrymen at the Gorsedda slate quarry in Eryri (SH 5606 4538). It is a planned settlement laid out on a grid pattern, and consists of detached cottages with a smallholding, so clearly of a rural character. Like the houses built by the Penrhyn Estate at Mynydd Landygai, the layout reflected the self-sufficient aspirations of its residents. Even

Small enclosures and the outline of houses make up the Ffos-y-Fran squatter settlement on the hill above Merthyr Tydfil, in a landscape surrounded by old ironstone workings.

A village in the Gwynedd hills. Treforys consisted of three parallel streets, with well-spaced cottages that have fallen to ruin.

Samaria is an early-nineteenth century quarryman's cottage
in Cilgwyn (Gwynedd), complete with its own small field.

Cwmorthin Calvinistic Methodist Chapel (Gwynedd) was built in 1867 and
drew its congregation from the local slate quarries above Blaenau Ffestiniog.
It closed for worship in the 1930s.

so, the settlement was ill-advised and the houses have long been abandoned, including a manager's house that was set further down the hillside on a site surrounded by trees. Conceived on a drawing board but positioned on an open, exposed hillside, it was probably always doomed to failure. The houses are now roofless and their walls no longer stand to full height, but a sense of the layout and its isolation is easy enough to appreciate. Cilgwyn (SH 495 540), above Nantlle, is a different kind of settlement. A squatter settlement on common land, it consists of homes built by the quarrymen themselves in the early–mid nineteenth century, using the materials they had to hand. It originated before the capitalist phase of slate quarrying reached the area. The layout is haphazard but you can see that workmen aspired to their own smallholding. Half of the village is now ruinous, following the closure of the nearby quarry in 1956. In the other half there remains a chapel building.

It takes more than houses to make a village. Schools, shops and places of worship are part of the mix that creates a local community. Nonconformist chapels can be associated with industrial settlement, like Cilgwyn mentioned above. The best-known 'upland' chapels are the ruins of two chapels associated with the scattered quarrymen's settlement at Cwmorthin on the hillside above Blaenau Ffestiniog. The Independent Chapel was built in 1866 (SH 6776 4601) and the Calvinistic Methodist Chapel in 1867, having previously functioned as a Sunday School (SH 6728 4640). The chapel was a vital part of rural Welsh life and, in sparsely populated districts, there were chapels in unlikely places. Tabor Independent Chapel was built above what is now Nant-y-Moch reservoir, inland from Aberystwyth. After it was demolished in 1998, the stone tablet from the front of the building was set up by the roadside as a memorial (SN 7364 8859). The lonely chapel of Soar y Mynydd, on the road from Tregaron to Llyn Brianne reservoir, was built in 1822 to serve a scattered upland population, and somehow survived the loss of potential members when a large tract of land was sold for forestry in the 1960s. The chapel is open for visitors and stands with a minister's house adjoining and a detached small stable, a feature it shares with the older remote parish churches.

Soar y Mynydd (Ceredigion) served a scattered rural population in a catchment area where Llyn Brianne reservoir was created in the 1970s. Against the odds, the chapel, its minister's house and a stable have survived.

Llangelynin, on the high plateau above the Conwy valley, is a medieval church that must always have served a scattered population.

A few churches are found on the fringes of open moorland, all of them on medieval sites. Llangelynin old church (SH 7512 7373), on the high plateau above the Conwy Valley, is a building no older than the fourteenth century, though it probably has earlier origins, and is one of the few churches to have a well in its churchyard. Llandecwyn Church (SH 6322 3762), with views out over Morfa Harlech and Porthmadog, perhaps owes its site to a former route over the mountains between the coast and Ffestiniog. The church was built in the late nineteenth century but it contains an inscribed stone of possibly the eleventh century and stands within an older rounded churchyard. Ysbyty Cynfan (SN 7524 7909) is a simple nineteenth-century church, but, as the 'ysbyty' element of its name implies, it was originally a medieval hospital used by pilgrims to St David's, and had been established by the Knights Hospitallers. Its churchyard wall includes three megaliths, for which reason it was once claimed to be (not very convincingly) the site of a stone circle.

7

UPLAND FARMING

M UCH of the archaeology of the uplands is concerned with farming. Despite the impression given by its often bleak, rocky and
boggy topography, there has been animal husbandry and arable farming on the uplands from prehistory to the twentieth century. Evidence
of upland farming is of special interest where it is found in abandoned
landscapes, because it can give a clearer picture of past farming and
settlement practice than the lowlands, where the landscape is more of
a palimpsest, on which modern centuries dominate.

The earliest farmers may have been no more than semi-nomadic
herders, moving their livestock across terrain according to the seasons. This kind of agriculture leaves no trace and the earliest evidence
on the ground of farming practices coincides with the earliest evidence of domestic life (in the later Bronze Age, increasing through
the Iron Age and into the Roman period). But it is evidence from the
medieval period onwards that dominates the archaeological record of
upland farming, over which time the extent of farming has been the
most significant factor determining what is now regarded as uplands.
The extent to which there is evidence of farming in the uplands has
in turn been determined by population pressures, changing economic
realities and even climate change. In the medieval and post-medieval
periods, for example, there have been periods when a shortage of land
has led people to farm on higher and higher ground, which has been
relinquished when such upland life was no longer desirable or viable.

Black Mountain Cottage is typical of the smallholdings found in the uplands of Radnorshire (Powys), a squatter cottage that became a smallholding, which has long since been abandoned.

Another factor that encouraged the search for land in the uplands was the custom of partible inheritance, or *gavelkind*, whereby a landholding was divided among all descendants equally, which could lead to a fragmentation of holdings to a scale too small to make them economically viable.

The climatic downturn of the late-thirteenth century, with consequent poor harvests, and the effects of plague in the mid-fourteenth century are factors that influenced retreat from the uplands. To that we can add the punitive measures taken against Wales following the Revolt of Owain Glyndŵr in the early fifteenth century, which affected the economy and population, and may, therefore, have led to a decline in upland settlement. But there were periods of advance in the twelfth and sixteenth centuries, creating a pattern of advance and retreat that ended with what seems like a permanent retreat in the late-nineteenth and twentieth centuries – a process that accelerated when the policy of free trade allowed large-scale imports of foodstuffs such as cereal crops from North America and meat from South America.

Landowners have also had a significant influence on the extent of upland farming. From the twelfth century there were monasteries actively developing the economy of Wales and its farming, and this spread to the uplands too. Cistercian monasteries such as Strata Florida (Ceredigion), Cwmhir (Powys) and Cymer (Gwynedd) were established in Wales – all with large estates covering land that was worth very little. The monasteries were active in economic development, establishing granges (outlying farms belonging to monasteries), even on high ground, that were let to tenant farmers. Where there is contemporary documentary evidence, the location of these granges can still be identified in the landscape in the form of later farmsteads, although these are now almost exclusively in enclosed ground and are no longer part of the mountain land.

Landowners have also had a significant impact on upland farming from the mid-eighteenth century. This coincided with competition from other interests, such as mineral exploitation and grouse shooting. Enclosure of unfenced hill land between 1750 and 1850 significantly reduced the amount of open hillside in Wales, to the extent that many upland parts of Wales were not included in the Right to Roam legislation of the early twenty-first century. It was also used by landowners to derive revenue from sheepwalks and was especially desirable where there were mineral rights at stake.

One of the special features of upland archaeology in the medieval and post-medieval periods is evidence of the movement of stock and people to the mountains in summer, known as transhumance in geography text books. We have already described the homesteads associated with this practice – *hendre, hafoty, lluest* – and their prevalence on Ordnance Survey maps. *Hafod* is the word that refers to the summer pasture (similar to the shielings of northern England), as opposed to the *hafoty* which refers only to the house. The other word that is associated with summer pastures is *ffridd* (plural *ffriddoedd*), a name that is often found on Ordnance Survey maps. Over time this has been a fairly flexible definition of pasture. It originally meant woodland or scrub, but later came to refer to upland cattle pasture and, later still, to sheep walks, although here it usually refers to enclosed ground immediately below the mountain wall.

Cattle, sheep and goats were the principal livestock herded on the mountain pastures. Dairy cattle were milked for making butter and cheese. In the transhumance economy, sheep were an all-rounder, in demand for their wool and as mutton, with the ewes milked for cheese and butter. The problems of leaving cattle and sheep on the mountain pastures over winter were twofold: the adverse weather conditions and the poor quality of natural winter feed. Goats are hardier than sheep and some of them lived semi-wild in the hills all year round, but even these were usually brought down for the winter. Goats were also a dairy animal, while dried goat was something of a speciality in North Wales. The hides could be sold on the market at a good price. The carcass produced a fine tallow for the best candles and, according to Thomas Pennant writing in the late-eighteenth century, the wool provided hair for wigs.

Transhumance thrived during the medieval period – John Leland described the *hafotai* of upland Ceredigion in the 1530s. It went into long-term decline from the sixteenth century, so that by the nineteenth century – the time from which there are published accounts of it – only vestiges remained of the former practice. One of the reasons for this was the decline of sheep as dairy animals and the focus on sheep as a source of wool. It therefore coincided with a period of transition from subsistence-based farming to specialist production of wool for sale to local factories.

Transhumance is an important symbol of pre-modern tradition, of a people attuned to nature and the cycle of the seasons. It is a farming practice in stark contrast to the zero-sum game of modern agriculture that began in the late-eighteenth century with the Board of Agriculture, which was not an official body but a pressure group of self-appointed agricultural improvers. That is a lens through which much of the writing about the practice of transhumance can be understood. One example is a classic and highly romanticised account of seasonal movement in Eryri published in 1812 by John Evans. During the summer months the farmers:

> leave their winter habitations, and take up residence in the hills; where they erect what are termed havodtai, or summer dairy houses ... Here the men pass their time tending their flocks, or in harvest work, while the women milk the cattle, and are occupied in their dairies.

If this was based on actual observations, it was contradicted by a survey conducted on behalf of the Board of Agriculture, a group that had little patience for the old traditional ways and wanted them swept aside in favour of more efficient modern methods. George Kay found that 'upon minute enquiry, I found no such custom existed' in his report on North Wales in 1794. The last days of transhumance lie somewhere between these two extreme accounts and the practice seems to have died out slowly. By the nineteenth century, sheep were still taken to the mountains for summer grazing, but the families no longer went with them and so they were left to the care of shepherds.

Transhumance was also practised in South Wales, but some of its upland pasture was suitable for year-round grazing. A survey of Hirwaun Common in 1660 noted that cattle were grazed on the common at all times of the year, and in the summer of 1803 Benjamin Malkin passed through this district and remembered hearing 'the voices of the herdsmen ranging over the mountains to collect their dispersed cattle at the approach of sunset'. These herdsmen would have looked out over the common to the blast furnaces smelting iron ore in Hirwaun, which had been in production for nearly 50 years by this time. Whether these were dairy cattle is not certain, but we know that women had traditionally travelled to the hills to carry out milking duties in the summer – in the accounts of the Margam Estate for 1719 and 1720 we find sums of £2 15 shillings and £3 paid to Mary Rees

The outline of early fields can be seen in this aerial view of the pass above the Conwy valley.

and her partners for milking 300 ewes over a period of three months on the hills above modern Port Talbot.

Radnorshire may also have seen all-round use of its unenclosed land. Here, there are large areas of common land but no very high peaks, and the terrain is generally less precipitous than other mountainous regions of Wales. The accessibility of the common lands was remarked upon by the Board of Agriculture's survey of Radnorshire in the early nineteenth century. It was claimed that farmers had a preference for upland farms on the fringes of the common rather than the fertile lowland farms, because the commons provided pasture that required no maintenance and demanded no rent. Rights to graze the commons were not universal and were generally confined to those farmsteads that bordered it. For the same reason it was reckoned in a Board of Agriculture Survey of South Wales, that at the end of the eighteenth century, 'a sheep-walk upon the mountains, attached to a farm, is of more value to the farmer than the farm itself'.

Remains of a small terrace cleared of loose stones, at an Iron Age farmstead near Bryn y Castell hillfort in Eryri (Gwynedd).

A small cairn field below Arenig Fawr (Gwynedd) was created to improve the land surface for agriculture, probably prehistoric in date.

Prehistoric and medieval fields and field systems can be found in many upland landscapes, usually associated with evidence of settlement. The characteristic that marks them out from later field systems is their relatively small size and associated settlement evidence. The easiest ones to identify consist of lines of fallen stones, although it is not clear how high these walls were originally built. Otherwise they are not easy to date, unless there are associated dateable features like prehistoric roundhouses, or medieval long huts, or place-names. State of preservation is a less reliable guide to date. Even so, if the wall is mainly covered in soil or peat then it is likely to be early. Early walls in upland landscapes do not follow a grid pattern but are likely to be of irregular shape with little emphasis on right angles. Undefended Iron Age settlements often have associated small fields for managing livestock. Other features to look for in the vicinity of round huts are areas where the ground has been cleared of stones – an indication that the land was ploughed for sowing crops, or where sloping ground has deliberately been terraced, again for planting crops. Where a larger area has been cleared of stones they are often gathered up into a series of small clearance cairns, known as a cairn field.

There are some well-preserved late-prehistoric and medieval field systems to be found in the Welsh mountains. There is a trackway, of prehistoric origin to judge from the megalithic sites along its route, and later a Roman road leading from the Conwy Valley across the hill country toward Caernarfon. On either side of the trackway is a complex network of small fields outlined by banks and walls, the latter representing the later use of the land (SH 738 716). Within this complex there are settlements of round huts, which are likely to be of late-Iron Age or Romano-British date, together with long huts of the medieval period, and post-medieval houses.

In the small valley of Cwm Pennant in the Berwyn Mountains, through which flows the small Afon Ceidiog (a tributary of the Dee), is evidence of medieval enclosures on the lower mountain slopes that represents the advance of farming in the medieval period from the flatter ground of the valley floor (SJ 047 332). These long, narrow strip fields, outlined by earthen banks, also overlie evidence of medieval ploughing and exist in a landscape where there are platforms of former houses on the hill slopes. These, of course, are not evidence of the *hafod* but of permanent settlement in the Middle Ages.

Visible boundaries in the uplands belong mostly to the post-medieval centuries, and likewise mostly belong to permanent farming, many of them as late as the nineteenth century. In the hendre/hafod system, the building of a summer house may have been one of the ways that a farmstead claimed its patch of the mountain land for summer grazing. There are no structures marking the boundaries though, perhaps because they were defined generally by natural features or older features like cairns. Although sheep were grazed on the uplands in the summer months, they did not roam endlessly over the mountain landscapes and nor did their shepherds want them to. Sheep range over a territory that they know – what farmers in North Wales called a *cynefin*. One of the reasons is that they keep together as a flock and like to know places to shelter when the weather is severe. The most important physical barrier was always the mountain wall that stopped sheep descending to the lusher lowland pastures. The non-physical division of hill pasture into sheep walks is indicated on some nineteenth-century tithe maps and estate maps. Physical traces belong to the eighteenth and mainly the nineteenth century, from the period when landowners had a vested interest in asserting ownership where there may have been valuable minerals, and as a way of charging rent. In Radnorshire there are some long low banks on the moorlands that show how the landscape was divided up, but more common are the stone walls that traverse long tracts of mountain land, many of which are included as access land. These have been strengthened in recent decades by wire fences, which is another, cheaper, way of dividing up large areas of hill pasture.

Field boundaries consist of banks, ditches and drystone walls. If not maintained, over time even stone walls will start to fall, earth accumulates over them and eventually they have the appearance of earthen banks. These may be early walls but their degradation is more a sign of when maintenance of them ceased. Earthen banks are less common, as would be expected in a landscape often littered with stones, and were often made by excavating a ditch alongside it.

Field walls are not uniform across upland Wales, and vary according to locality and the types of stone available. Look at the make-up of stone walls and they will appear mostly to be of stones gathered from the ground. You can find, however, small quarried outcrops close to walls that are another clue to the source of the stone used. So the appearance can differ from walls that look professionally built because the stone

Lluest Pen Rhiw (Powys), above the Wye valley in mid Wales, was a medieval summer dwelling that became a permanent farmstead, after which the large enclosure was created on the open hill.

Old stone walls, like this example near Llanarmon Dyffryn Ceiriog (Wrexham), are often now partly turf-covered.

If the right shape, boulders are often raised upright as gate piers (Gwynedd).

Slate fences, this example by Llyn Cwmorthin (Gwynedd), are characteristic of the slate-working district of North Wales.

A distinctive North Wales wall of field stones near Llyn Ogwen, Eryri (Gwynedd).

A field wall of pitched slabs near Rhayader (Powys).

naturally occurs in regular shapes, to walls that look amateurish, but are in fact just the result of using found stones of random shapes and sizes. In South Wales, for example, the local Pennant sandstone occurs in quite thin beds, which is reflected in the regular courses of the walls here. In most of North Wales the walls are constructed of found stones and are therefore less regular in appearance. One type of stone wall specific to locality is the slate fence found in North Wales. Slate breaks into relatively thin slabs which are laid on end in lines and are found in the slate-quarrying areas of Eryri, sometimes held together with wire threaded through them. All sorts of other creative uses were found for slate, which include gate piers and smaller enclosures like the pens attached to pigsties.

In a drystone wall, or any wall for that matter, the largest stones are usually found at the base, and are known as boulder footings. The top course is known as the coping and is usually made distinctive by laying the stones on end. Gate piers are often formed of single large uprights, or even boulders, where they are easily available (and have sometimes been mistaken for prehistoric standing stones). Other associated features include sheep creeps, described below, and corbelled steps as primitive 'step stiles'.

As sheep farming has dominated the upland economy, especially over recent centuries, it has left the greatest quantity of archaeological features. The management of sheep on the uplands was not uniform across Wales. In north-west Wales, where the rock-strewn landscape provided plenty of building material, the sheepfold is the signature feature of hill farming, but in other parts of Wales they are much less common. In Ceredigion, for example, the upland farmers traditionally built their folds of underwood and furze, like hurdles, rather than as permanent stone structures.

The majority of sheepfolds probably belong to the eighteenth and nineteenth centuries, and all of them are marked on the county-series Ordnance Survey maps from the late nineteenth century onwards. Some of them are re-used and/or adapted older structures such as houses. In North Wales you can find sub-circular folds and sub-rectangular folds,

A large enclosure with small fold, makes the most of the natural topography in Eryri (Gwynedd).

but it is not certain that the rounded structures are necessarily earlier. The classic position for a sheepfold is in a sheltered position, often at the base of a hill, sometimes integrated with a field wall, sometimes against natural cliffs, which reduces the effort to build them. They also needed to be relatively accessible and there are even some that are attached to upland farmsteads. Perhaps the best example is at Cwm Bychan farm by Llyn Cwm Bychan in Ardudwy (SH 6469 3151), which also has a stone carved with 'EVANLL', referring to Evan Lloyd who died in 1785. These traditional sheepfolds were used well into the twentieth century but are no longer in use. Where the sheep have to be gathered – when they are dipped for example – farmers have developed simpler and more flexible systems using metal fences.

Sheepfolds were used for all the differing needs of the hill farmers – to gather and sort sheep, to prepare for shearing or washing, to keep sheep that have strayed from their allotted pasture, for milking ewes,

A simple sheepfold is built against the side of an exposed rock face in Eryri (Gwynedd).

for penning lambs when they were first born (confining the ewes at this time is important for efficiently milking them) and simply to provide shelter in exposed landscapes. There were various reasons why sheep needed to be sorted: for example, if several flocks grazed the same tract of land, for sorting out the lambs for bringing down the mountain for sale or for their winter quarters. At one time, the wethers (the castrated male sheep) could be left on the mountains in winter, but their numbers declined when the public taste shifted from mutton to lamb.

Single-cell sheepfolds were useful for milking the ewes and for gathering small flocks. Raised stances within them were for placing the ewes to make it easier to milk them. Small bays were used for penning the ewes and lambs, which may incorporate a small roofed shelter for protection of the lambs. Multi-celled sheepfolds indicate a step change in the scale of sheep rearing and were useful for sorting out sheep. These could have grown incrementally from simpler folds as the requirements for sheep management changed. They are built around a large gathering fold, with smaller pens attached. In places where a sheep walk was used by multiple farms, each of the pens might be reserved for the flocks of individual farms or smallholdings.

A multi-celled sheepfold in Eryri (Gwynedd), with guide walls to direct sheep on to the hill.

This two-cell sheepfold in Gwynedd has an opening to a stream,
evidence that it was used as a sheep wash.

Sheep were gathered in midsummer and washed in local streams before they were sheared, a practice that continued well into the twentieth century. First of all, the sheep needed to be gathered in folds, which also allowed checks on their general health. These sheepfolds are easy to identify because they are close to streams. The accompanying sheep washes are also easy to identify because the fold has a gate that opens to the stream or river and are usually located at a point where a natural pool was formed. Failing that, it was possible to partially dam a watercourse to create the necessary depth of water. The sheep were sheared when dry, with their legs tied. Sheep are no longer treated the same way before shearing, and sheep washes are not to be confused with sheep dips, which use strong chemicals to kill parasites and involve a process carried out in enclosed tanks.

Other features to look out for are sheep creeps, which are low apertures in the walls that allowed sheep to pass through; and guide walls attached to the outside of the fold, which directed the sheep a certain way when they left it. They were thus used to control the movement of sheep back on to the hill.

A simple sheep creep.

A short wall used as a shelter for sheep.

A shelter wall in Eryri (Gwynedd) that could be used by shepherds,
peat-cutters, hikers or sheep.

Stone shelter built against a natural outcrop.

This shelter near Capel Curig (Conwy) has been documented as a *cwt myn*, a kids' hut used when milking goats. Similar structures were also used for milking ewes.

Sheep shelters on the open hillside are simple walls that allow the sheep to shelter in inclement weather but they are found only occasionally. The natural topography and its rocky surface means that the mountains of Wales have plenty of natural shelters that animals will find. In Merioneth, some cross-plan walls were erected so that shelter could be had whichever way the prevailing weather was driven, while on the hills above Llanllechid in Gwynedd Lord Penrhyn was said to have erected sheds for sheep. In practice, though, expect to find only simple walls used for shelter.

Shepherds also needed to take shelter, often in pre-existing buildings, such as abandoned *hafotai*, but there are small, rudimentary huts that were originally roofed, that shepherds either built or used. Those with evidence of a fireplace self-evidently belong to recent centuries, but those without are not necessarily any older. A fire in a shepherd's hut was a luxury, but fireplaces also had a more practical purpose in melting pitch to brand sheep and to treat them if they had foot rot. Cwt Jacob (SH 6675 6895) is a rare example of a shepherd's hut that can be linked with an individual shepherd. The hut, complete with a hearth and chimney, stands close to three sheepfolds and was built *c.*1900 by Jacob Zack, who looked after the flock of sheep belonging to Glyn Farm, Abergwyngregyn. In the hills inland of Tywyn there is a large sheepfold above Dolgoch (SH 6664 0341) which incorporates a fireplace and flue for melting pitch.

Even more primitive than huts are the shelters built by shepherds, as well as peat-cutters, game keepers and industrial workmen (and in some individual cases were perhaps shared by all four). These self-built, usually drystone structures make use of any natural features such as rock outcrops so as to keep out the worst of the driving rain. They could also be used by sheep and goats, of course. Most of the surviving examples probably date from the post-medieval centuries, and shelter-builders have been no respecters of earlier archaeology. It is not uncommon to find prehistoric cairns in which the stones have been re-formed to create a crude shelter. Some of these shelters are very recent. On the hillside above Bwlch Oerddrws, between Dinas

Mawddwy and Dolgellau, are numerous crude shelters. These were not built by walkers, but by plane spotters, waiting on the hillside to photograph low-flying military aircraft that pass through on what is described as the Mach Loop.

The archaeology of goat husbandry is more limited because mountain goats lived semi-wild on the hills. The shelters and small folds that were used for milking ewes could equally have been used for milking goats. There are specific examples of small roofed pens (known in Eryri as a *cwt myn* or kids' hut) which are said to have been constructed specifically for milking goats, although in appearance they are the same as those associated with milking ewes. A well-documented example is above the A5 near Capel Curig (SH 7188 5916). Another rare type of site is the fox trap. One is incorporated into a sheepfold in a clearing near Dolgellau (SH 6949 1981), which has walls 2.5m high, conspicuously high for a fold, which are corbelled inwards at the top to prevent a fox from jumping out.

Cattle farming has left much less clear evidence in the landscape. A common feature of north-west Wales is the field cow house, known as a *beudy*, which is found regularly in the landscapes of Eryri, within enclosed (as well as the higher, unenclosed) ground. These are of post-medieval date and were useful as a means of keeping cattle on the hills for a greater proportion of the year than was formerly the practice, and so post-date the traditional seasonal movement of animals. Thomas Rowlandson gave a valuable description in 1847 of how the *beudy* functioned in practice. A farmstead might have several of them set at a suitable distance from each other. They were large enough to accommodate up to eight cattle, and each *beudy* had a small stack yard. These buildings are quite uniform and easy to identify. The doorway is in the gable end of the building and the yard is attached to the opposite gable end which, if the walls stand anything like their full height, will have a pitching hole for forking the hay through. The main entrance is on the downhill end of the building, which made the mucking-out easier. For this reason they are easy to distinguish from habitations, which usually had the doorway in the long wall. A common feature is

A *beudy*, with stack yard, above Cwmystradllyn in Gwynedd.

that the *beudy* is very well-built (perhaps professionally) but the construction of the adjoining yard is rougher.

Horses, rabbits and geese have also been reared on the mountains. Of these, horses have left no discernible archaeology. According to Walter Davies, writing in 1810, ponies were reared on the mountain pastures all year round in Merioneth and neighbouring Montgomeryshire. Known locally as *merlins*, they were driven down from the hills to the fairs when they were three years old. There have also been wild ponies on the hills for centuries, although their numbers have been in long-term decline. The Carneddau ponies of Eryri are rounded up by the local farmers once a year for health checks. They clip the ponies' tails before setting them free again, so if you see one with a long tail it is one of the elusive ones that has evaded the farmers. The Carneddau ponies are slightly smaller than the more-common Section A Mountain Ponies that are found across mid and South Wales, which are semi-feral and have been designated as a rare breed.

Rabbit warrens became part of the upland landscape in the medieval period, but most of the evidence you will find is probably much later. The ready-made warrens were intended to attract breeding rabbits, and are housed in specially-constructed earthworks known as pillow mounds, which are commonly found in the uplands of mid Wales. Historically these have often acquired names like Giant's Grave or Soldiers Graves. Superficially they may look like long barrows but they rarely rise above 1m in height, and can be anything from 5m to 20m long. Their other distinguishing feature is that they are usually found on sloping ground with a rounded lower end and a surrounding ditch. Round mounds are sometimes associated with larger groups of pillow mounds, and were usually 'trap mounds'. These small mounds had a central post with a trap mounted on it, which was used to ensnare predators such as buzzards who would naturally seek out a perch while looking for prey. Pillow mounds can be found in enclosed land but they are also occasionally found on the unenclosed mountain and common lands. There are some large upland groups, like those on Mynydd Lluestcethingrych in Montgomeryshire (SH 862 002), and

A pillow mound on the Radnorshire commons (Powys).

Pant Mawr, Ystradfellte in the Bannau Brycheiniog National Park (SN 905 143). Isolated pillow mounds are also a feature of the uplands, especially in Radnorshire, where they are associated with cottages, smallholdings and *tai-unnos*. On these poor uplands the cottagers supplemented their incomes by breeding rabbits for their meat and skin.

Throughout history the moorlands have been used primarily for pasture, but not exclusively so. Before foodstuffs and fertilisers could be transported efficiently across the country, mixed farming was the norm, even in the marginal upland landscapes. These communities were substantially self-sufficient before the twentieth century, so upland communities relied on what they could grow for cereals and vegetables, with fruit picked and fish caught in season. In 1798 Richard Warner described the people of Merioneth as subsisting on a diet of little meat, but oaten cake (unfermented bread), bread made from a mixture of wheat and rye, cheese, potatoes and butter-milk. Other travellers of the era noted the local character of the cuisine. At Eisteddfa Gurig, not so remote now that it is on the main road to Aberystwyth, Leitch Ritchie found, during his 'pedestrian ramble' of the River Wye in the 1830s, barley cakes, beef, salted sow and mutton, all slaughtered at home. In Llangurig two decades later, Thomas Roscoe thought the bread had a distinct peaty flavour. He also noticed that, in his admiration of the 'cheerful, hard-feeding mountaineers' of Ceredigion, that the flummery (apparently a sour jelly made from oat-husks), buttermilk and coarse barley bread was the diet of poor people. As for drinks, milk or butter-milk mixed with water was common, beer less so in areas where little barley and no hops were grown, although it always seems to have been available to visitors.

Contemporary accounts of the late-eighteenth and early-nineteenth century emphasise that there were no ploughs on the hill farms; that the soil was dug over using a spade, and that wheeled vehicles were scarce – produce being moved around on sleds; manure in barrows. Only the hardier cereal crops were grown in the uplands – especially oats, but also barley and rye (rye bread was an important part of the diet in much of rural Wales until the nineteenth century). Rye, sown in September or October for harvesting the following summer, was an excellent grain for cultivating on poor, acid soils (the application of lime had a negative effect on a crop of rye – one of the reasons it declined in importance). *Rhyd du*, or dusky rye, was the type most commonly sown in upland terrain, and there was the added advantage that rye bread kept better in summer than wheat bread. Oats were an all-rounder and were grown in all conditions in Wales, with the added advantage that its straw provided much better fodder for cattle than rye straw.

As we have seen, some farmsteads, especially in North Wales, milled their own cereal crops, which could be intended for winter livestock feed as well as human consumption. Vegetables were grown in smaller plots. Potatoes, turnips (used as animal feed) and peas were commonly grown in the early nineteenth century, especially on common land where small areas could be ploughed informally. In 1803 Benjamin Malkin saw 'stripes and patches of cultivation scattered over the prevailing nakedness' of the commons in Radnorshire. In 1815 Walter Davies quoted an account of how potatoes were grown on marginal bracken-infested soil in lazy beds:

fern, where plentiful, were cut green in June or July, and laid thick on the sward intended for potatoes. In March or April following, the sward, roots and all, would be entirely rotted, and the soil as mellow as that of a garden. The fern were turned over the breadth of the intended trench; the potatoes set on the fern, and mould thrown from the trenches to cover the lazy beds.

This was regarded as a very efficient way of using the 'coarse sidelands'. Potatoes were grown on some of the upland commons in wartime, a good example of how many farming practices in the uplands were episodic, responding in times of need and then being abandoned in the better times.

Some of the natural vegetation was also harvested for human use, although you will never find evidence of it now. Gorse bushes were cut for cleaning chimneys and shoes. Bracken was cut to provide bedding

These narrow corrugations on the Preseli Hills are probably the remains of potato farming in the war years.

for farm animals, and occasionally for use as thatch or to provide potash. In some areas molina hay was cut for fodder. Known in mid Wales as *gwair cwta*, or rhos hay, the practice continued in some areas as late as the 1970s.

Enclosed fields are likely to have been sown with crops if it is apparent that they have been cleared of stones. Sometimes these occur as terraces on sloping ground, known to archaeologists as lynchets, although they can be difficult to identify. Otherwise, evidence of arable farming in the uplands is most likely to survive in the form of 'ridge and furrow'. These are linear corrugations in the ground which result from growing crops in strips. It was how crop-rearing in the lowlands was organised in Wales, though not in the open-field system familiar in the flatter parts of southern and eastern England. The direction of the corrugations is always up and down the slope – the problem of digging the ground across the slope is that it inhibits drainage from the furrows. The width of the corrugations will give you some indication of the kind of crops that were grown. Narrow ridge and furrow is usually the result of growing potatoes, and the wider furrows, which have ridges up to 2m wide, are evidence of cereal cultivation.

A large area of ridge and furrow on common land in Radnorshire is of medieval or post-medieval date.

Ridge and furrow is not easy to date by itself, although it is notable how rarely the evidence is contained within field walls. An example of where ridge and furrow underlies medieval field boundaries in Cwm Pennant has already been described. This does not mean that they represent evidence of medieval arable farming, although the uplands were certainly suitable for growing crops until the climatic deterioration of the mid-fourteenth century, and in later centuries too. The usual arrangement was for the crops to be grown on the lowest of the mountain land with the upper contours reserved for sheep and goats. However, in Eryri, ridge and furrow can be found on quite steep ground, often covering irregular patches of ground, simply because ground free of outcropping rocks that could be dug over was hard to find. In Radnorshire ridge and furrow can extend over large tracts of common land and is one of the most satisfying archaeological features to identify.

8

INDUSTRIAL SITES

WALES is a land of great natural resources, in the form of the water that falls on it and the stone that lies beneath it. These have been exploited across the uplands, and in many areas they form the dominant feature of the archaeological landscape. Exploitation of raw materials is not a recent phenomenon in Wales, but it accelerated exponentially during the Industrial Revolution, so expect most industrial remains to belong to the eighteenth and nineteenth centuries. Find one industrial feature and there will probably be others close by, so that industrial archaeology usually survives as a complex of features. This general rule becomes more apparent for more recent centuries as the scale of exploitation increased – the large-scale iron and coal industries of South Wales and the slate industry of North Wales produced what are best described as industrial landscapes.

The key to identifying what kind of industry a site is associated with is geography. If you are in South Wales it is mainly coal and ironworking; in mid and North Wales, metal mining; and, especially in northwest Wales, slate quarrying and mining. Limestone quarries are found in many parts of Wales, an indication of which is the presence of lime kilns. Earthwork features on peaty moorland are likely to be peat cuttings. Wales is a landscape of hard rocks, and stone was quarried from across upland Wales to provide building materials.

Many of the industries described here are not associated exclusively with upland landscapes. Raw materials were extracted from the most convenient place, which more often than not was in lowland land-scapes, and the success of these industries also often depended upon accessibility to transport systems. For example, when coal was mined from deep underground the collieries no longer needed to be sunk where the coal seams break the surface. So, after 1850, the railway came to be a determining factor in the siting of collieries, and railways prefer level landscapes where possible. However, unlike coal which can be won from very deep underground, slate was quarried or mined from the surface or just below it, so in this case geology was the deter-mining factor. The uplands remain the best place to discover remains of the slate industry, from the medieval period to the mid-twentieth century.

GATHERING FIELD STONES

Geologists classify the age of rocks by reference to Wales and its geol-ogy – the Cambrian and pre-Cambrian ages – and its stones have been

This gable end of a farm building in Eryri (Gwynedd) is a good examples of the use field stones gathered from the ground, with the large stones at the base.

exploited for building in just about every part of the country. But when we talk about quarry-ing in Wales, we mean stone won from solid bedrock as well as stone collected from the ground. The last Ice Age covered nearly all of the land mass of Wales and beneath it debris was carried along, scraping away the ground surface and leaving, when the ice finally melted, a landscape lit-tered with loose stones. In many parts of the uplands, the ground is still strewn with loose rocks, but most of it has been cleared to remove impediments, or gath-ered as a free building material.

A fireplace in a quarry barracks is built mostly of quarried stone, much of it dressed to give a smooth face.

The biggest surface stones are known as erratics, some of which were raised upright as prehistoric standing stones, or were adopted as boundary markers, but they can also be found embedded into field walls. Few, if any of them seem to have moved any distance at all, but even smaller stones seem to have been used more or less where they were collected. Glacial erratics are possible to identify because they have been carried along under the ice and so differ from the immediate underlying geology. But, in general, the stone walls and buildings of the Welsh uplands are as good a guide to the underlying geology of Wales as any map.

Clearing the ground of stone had multiple benefits – it provided a better surface for grazing animals, land that could be dug over and sown with crops and was an easy quarry for building stone. Look at field walls and buildings and the shape of the stones give some indication of how the material was obtained. Field stones were subject to weathering and so naturally have a rounded appearance, whereas quarried stone is freshly broken up and has sharper, more distinct edges. In practice, of course, stones collected from the ground also often needed to be split to make them easier to use.

Prehistoric Quarries

We know that there were quarries in prehistoric times, since there are at least two quarries in Wales where the stones were used for more than local purposes. On the Preseli Hills in Pembrokeshire is a series of outcrops of spotted dolerite, a very hard stone that has a blue tinge when split, hence its alternative name of bluestone. Stone from these hills was transported to Salisbury Plain where it formed the rings of stones in one of the early incarnations of Stonehenge. It was difficult enough to transport stones from the Preseli hills, probably along the course of the Bristol Channel, which at that time of lower sea level was still partly the valley of the River Severn, but the precise sources chosen were hardly the most practical. Detailed petrological analysis has identified the precise source of these stones as Carn Goedog (SN 129 332). It is one of several outcrops along the ridge of the Preseli Hills, where the bedrock is naturally split into monolith-shaped blocks. Carn Goedog has been identified as the quarry, although whether there were suitable loose blocks of stone on the surface, or whether it had to be hewn from the bedrock is uncertain. It is also possible that the bluestones were first erected in a stone circle near their source before they were later transported to Salisbury Plain.

Carn Goedog in the Preseli Hills (Pembrokeshire) is the source of the bluestones used at Stonehenge.

Craig Lwyd, Penmaenmawr (SH 719 753), was quarried for the manufacture of stone tools and was one of the largest Neolithic axe factories in Britain. Polished axes from the site were traded across a large part of Britain, and have been found as far afield as Kent and Yorkshire, with a concentration in Wiltshire. The igneous rock was exploited from natural outcrops and scree material. On the quarry sites, the stones were flaked to produce 'roughouts', pieces of manageable size that could then be worked into the precise size and shape, and then polished, on separate sites. Some of the waste from this process was uncovered in excavations of 1919–21. Much of Craig Lwyd has been subject to quarrying in the nineteenth and twentieth centuries, when its stone was in demand for making granite setts, railway ballast and road stone, and it remains an active site. Quarrying is a destructive business, which, by its nature, destroys evidence of earlier workings. Evidence of this important early mining activity is now indirect, in the form of the 'Druids Circle' stone circle and associated megalithic monuments on the plateau immediately south, and the trackway along which the material was transported.

Quarries for building stone

In most parts of Wales you will find quarries for building stone. The majority of them provided stone only for local use. The reason for this is its quality – although suitable for rubble-stone construction, Wales has little in the way of freestone that can be used for carved decoration, much of which on Welsh buildings has been imported. Even the most unpromising bedrock, the gravel derived from friable beds of shale, has been exploited to provide aggregate for concrete. In parts of mid Wales shale was crushed to form a clay used in brick-making. Although it is usually associated with lowland valleys, there are also gravel pits in the Welsh hills, especially in the Clwydian range. Slate was the first Welsh stone to find a national market, followed in the twentieth century by the hard dolerites found in North Wales which are quarried to provide railway ballast and stone paving, as at Penmaenmawr described above.

Local geology makes an enormous contribution to the regional character of Welsh buildings. In South Wales, there are buildings of grey Pennant sandstone, that came from quarries in the upper and middle coal measures. Pennant sandstone is particularly intractable and was split along its natural seams. The result is that many buildings are constructed of relatively thin blocks of stone, which might look like a design feature but is in fact the only way it could be used in practice. In Breconshire there is the distinctive red sandstone, while in north-west Wales the grey and grey-purple tones of slate predominate; but even here there are subtle differences in the hue and texture of slate from the south and north parts of Eryri. Slate, before it became associated with the thin roofing materials quarried from North Wales, was used to describe any stones that could be split into thin-enough pieces to be used as a roofing material. So it can refer to other types of sandstone that could be split to provide stone roof tiles, a common sight in the Breconshire district of Powys.

Quarrying is not a specifically upland industry. Stone was normally quarried as close to its intended building site as possible, which means that in the sparsely-built uplands small quarries are the norm. Quarries are by their nature very difficult to date, except by association. And some of the earliest quarries will not have survived because later workings by definition obliterate evidence of earlier working. Ordnance Survey maps show only the larger quarries, but the earlier county-series at the 6-inch scale show just how commonplace they are in the landscape. Small areas of quarrying can be recognised where there is a vertical, unnatural-looking face, with a levelled area in front. The most convenient location to quarry stone was often a roadside outcrop, so it is not unusual to find rectangular cuts into bedrock, which are sometimes now opportune places to park a car. The stone for building the Caban Coch dam in the Elan Valley and Elan village was hewn from Gigfran Quarry (SN 9240 6459), now resurrected as the Caban Coch car park above the reservoir dam.

Where do I find the larger quarries? Apart from slate, where the material was both quarried and dressed on site, the largest quarries are

The long quarry face at Trefor Rocks in the Dee Valley near Llangollen.

found in South Wales. Quarrying went hand-in-hand with the iron and coal industry because large quantities of stone were needed for ironworks, colliery buildings and colliery villages. At Abergorky in the Rhondda Fawr there are large quarries on the hillside above the former colliery site and the village (ss 961 986), which were probably obvious candidates for exploitation because they had exposed outcrops, though it was unusual for such large quarries to be on steep ground. Here, quarried sandstone was lowered down the hillsides by means of inclined planes, in part using colliery waste as a counterweight, allowing the stone to be moved downhill and the waste to be moved to hillside slag tips. Abergorky has quarry faces up to 15m high and a line of quarry tips on the downhill side, but the post-industrial regrading of the landscape has obscured some of the detail, including the inclined planes. At Trefor Rocks near Llangollen (sj 228 433), the exposed limestone cliffs were exploited in the nineteenth century, and are easy to identify as quarry faces because there are spoil mounds at the base of the cliffs and the lines of former railways serving them have survived as paths.

Sedimentary rocks predominate in Wales, mostly sandstone but also significant reserves of carboniferous limestone, which can be used for building (especially in north-east Wales) but has other industrial uses. When burned, limestone produced a white powder, known as lime, which was used for whitewashing buildings, as a mortar in construction, and was spread over fields to neutralise acid soils. Its latter use provided a market which extended beyond Wales, evidence of which is the number of lime kilns to be found around the coast that thrived in the pre-railway age. In the iron industry large quantities of limestone were needed as a flux for the smelting process, and were added to the coke and iron ore in the blast furnaces. Limestone quarries are mainly found just north of the valleys, which in practice means north of the Heads of the Valleys Road and at the south end of the Bannau Brycheiniog National Park.

A small-scale limestone quarry at Foel Fawr in the Black Mountains (Carmarthenshire).

A large area of nineteenth-century limestone quarries, disused by the end of the century, can be found near Penderyn in the Bannau Brycheiniog National Park (Powys). It has earthwork remains of old lime kilns.

There is lots of evidence that the burning of lime was a small-scale, perhaps even sporadic, occupation. For example, on the common ground of the Breconshire uplands north of Rhymney, there are small quarries with adjacent kilns. These were probably the work of single or small groups of commoners, who took away their burnt lime by pack-horse. Writing in his *History of Brecknock* in 1809 Theophilus Jones described a once thriving lime-burning industry with kilns on the unenclosed uplands, examples of which can be seen on Cefn yr Ystrad, with adjoining small quarries (for example at SO 0934 1389). The opening of the Brecknock and Abergavenny Canal, and the construction of tramroads to access it, stimulated larger-scale quarrying on these hills in the nineteenth century. The Bryn Oer tramroad was built in 1815, from the Union Ironworks near Rhymney to the Brecknock and Abergavenny Canal, and passes close to the limestone quarries of Cefn yr Ystrad. Local entrepreneurs seized their opportunity. The Blaen

Dyffryn Crawnon lime works, with lime kilns (SO 1000 1513), survives facing the former tramroad. These works were later dwarfed by the twentieth-century workings described below.

Lime kilns are simple structures, usually built in pairs or multiples. Almost invariably they are built against a natural bank, which allowed the layers of limestone and coal to be charged from the top. The contents of the kiln were burned very slowly, over a period of days. The white lime was drawn out at the base of the kiln, where the draw hole was placed within an arched recess. The recess allowed some protection from gusts of wind, helpful when the product of the kiln was essentially a powder. These kilns are cased in stone, with finely-built stone arches. Easy to identify, they are sometimes found by the quarries themselves, but are otherwise located next to old tramroads or canals.

There is a fine and well-preserved series of quarries and lime kilns at Foel Fawr on the Black Mountain in Carmarthenshire, known collectively as the Black Mountain Quarries (SN 733 189). Quarrying

A large twentieth-century limestone quarry at Foel Fawr (Carmarthenshire), with lime kiln.

began here when the road (now the A4069) over the Black Mountain between Brynamman and Llangadog was built in 1819. Quarrying and lime burning already had a long history here as it was exploited by local farmers on common land, but in the nineteenth century several enterprises introduced industrial-scale working. Most of the quarries belong to this period, but there was also a revival of the quarries in the twentieth century, from which period there are several well-preserved large lime kilns.

The other very large-scale workings in South Wales is at Trefil (SO 086 145), north of Rhymney, where some of the evidence of small nineteenth-century workings has been obliterated. This huge quarry, re-opened in the second half of the twentieth century, is now a landscape of deep pits – up to 40m deep and some of them flooded – with remains of crushing and screening plants and a network of service roads with street lighting powered by the quarry's own electricity sub-station.

For upland limestone quarries that supplied the iron industry, head to the Blaenavon World Heritage Site. The limestone quarries are all on the north side of the coal measures, on slopes looking to the north and the Black Mountains beyond Abergavenny. The quarry at Pwll Du (SO 251 116) is well integrated into the landscape of the Blaenavon ironworks. Limestone was taken south to the blast furnaces at Blaenavon, at first by the narrow road that still crosses the moorland above the quarry. In 1817 a horse-drawn tramroad, known as Hill's Tramroad, was opened, making transport easier and connecting with the Brecknock and Abergavenny Canal at Govilon. Later still, a railway incline, known as Dyne Steel Incline, brought limestone to the blast furnaces. Pwll Du is an unusual quarry because the limestone had to be transported uphill away from the quarry rather than downhill. The answer was to build a water-balance lift, similar to those used to raise coal in the early collieries. This was fed by a large pond which survives on the upper side of the quarry (SO 2519 1137).

In the Blaenavon landscape as a whole, which includes the Blorenge, the chronology of limestone quarrying is preserved at several sites which

Nineteenth-century quarry and lime kilns at Rhes-y-Cae on Halkyn Mountain (Flintshire).

show how the industry, especially in terms of scale, developed. Early small-scale workings are found on the north side of the Blorenge (for example at SO 2688 1240), with an associated tramroad built c.1796 to carry the stone to the furnaces. The Tyla quarries on the east side of Gilwern Hill (SO 247 125) are larger and later than Pwll Du, and they also provided Blaenavon ironworks with limestone via the Hill's Tramroad. Further west are the Clydach lime works (SO 234 128), a large-scale quarry of late-nineteenth and twentieth-century workings with associated features like railway sidings and lime kilns.

A completely different landscape character can be found on Halkyn Mountain, Flintshire, where limestone was also exploited in the nineteenth century and where there are numerous small quarries and lime kilns. In 1796 Thomas Pennant had remarked that the local grey limestone was particularly suited to manufacturing hydraulic cement,

This partially restored lime kiln for 'aberdo' on Halkyn Mountain (Flintshire) shows the brick lining of the kiln that was charged with coal and limestone from the top, and where the burnt lime was dug out from the bottom.

which sets in wet conditions and was in demand for the building of docks in the nineteenth century. There are several lime kilns associated with the cement industry (SJ 1859 7317), but also lime kilns associated with small quarries where the rock was hewn using only hand tools like crow bars and wedges.

Peat cutting

Until the nineteenth century peat heated the homes of people living across large swathes of Wales. Peat is mainly, but not exclusively, an upland phenomenon – there were important lowland sources of peat near Tregaron and Borth, the latter being a significant source of fuel for Aberystwyth. Its use gradually declined after the railways spread across rural Wales, allowing coal to be transported cheaply. At the same time more open land was enclosed, reducing the areas where people had a right to dig turves. In the twentieth century afforestation reduced further the available peat lands. But in the more remote areas, tenants in hill farms and shepherds' huts still relied on peat as they had limited access to coal. They also felt they were entitled to it. This was highlighted in 1902, when it was proposed to curtail peat-cutting rights on Birmingham Corporation's mountain land above the Elan Valley. One local landowner pointed out that the right to cut peat 'is a valuable right to me, and my tenants … and also the Shepherd who has a house on the Llyest, where he would be entirely dependent on turf for fuel.' Before the dams were built, farmers in the Elan Valley would go up on to the hills in spring, spend a week cutting and stacking turves, then leave them to dry until they were brought down in September – a pattern, and part of the rural calendar, repeated across much of upland Wales.

An area of peat cutting is known as a turbary, and many of them were documented by travellers passing over the uplands in the eighteenth and nineteenth centuries. Thomas Pennant, passing through the Vale of Mawddwy in the 1770s, provides us with a valuable account of the laborious and time-consuming methods of acquiring and bringing down such a heavy and bulky material from the hills:

The turberries [sic] are placed very remote from their dwellings; and the turf or peat is gotten with great difficulty. The roads from the brows of the mountains, in general, are too steep even for a horse; the men therefore carry up on their backs, a light sledge, fill it with a very considerable load, and drag it, by means of a rope placed over their breast, to the brink of the slope; then go before, and draw it down, still preceding, and guiding its motions, which at times have been so violent, as to overturn and draw along with it the master, to the hazard of his life, and not without considerable bodily hurt.

The sledge was called a *glwyd-fawn*, or 'hurdle', and was about 5 feet long, in use at a time when farmers had few wheeled vehicles and regularly used sleds for farm work. Other contemporary accounts describe how the use of sleds to transport bulky and heavy material eroded the tracks and led to the creation of braided trackways, although definitive evidence of braiding is no longer visible.

Spotting evidence of former peat cuttings is quite difficult. Although cutting was done systematically, leaving straight edges, the material is fragile and the straight lines can quickly erode. I have had farmers point out to me areas where peat was cut within living memory, but where there is no visible evidence that a spade has been anywhere near. Although there are places where a rectangular depression clearly represents old cuttings, the evidence of former peat cutting is usually found in the form of associated features.

The first thing to be aware of is the general areas where peat could be cut. These are usually relatively flat and boggy. Place-names can also help – the suffix *fawnog*, meaning a place of peat, is a good if not fail-safe indicator. Peat needs to be carried away from the hills and so the presence of a track that enters then peters out in moorland is a clue (assuming it does not lead to a sheepfold). The right to dig peat was one of the commoners rights, but, in strict legal terms, peat was supposed to be dug from within the parish boundary. That these laws were unenforced, and unenforceable, is evidenced by trackways, shown on the county-series Ordnance Survey maps, that lead to the turbaries above Pennant Melangell (Powys) and clearly extend into the neighbouring parish of Llandrillo (Denbighshire).

After cutting, peat was stacked to let it dry. Rectangular platforms with surrounding gullies were constructed on which to stack the peat, around which timber posts were once placed so as to deter stock from knocking the peat over, as revealed by excavation rather than survival above ground. There are places where peat was cut and stacked, but never retrieved, like the Beddau Gwyr Ardudwy near Llan Ffestiniog (SH 7230 4258), already described. Other raised platforms are identifiable as a kerb of stones, often oval in shape and on sloping ground that had natural drainage (also known as peat stools), or even a platform of loose stones. There is a dense concentration of peat stands in the Vale of Mawddwy, in a landscape where evidence of the cuttings themselves is elusive.

Rarer still are peat houses, found occasionally in north-west Wales. These were of simple drystone constructions, windowless, with slab

These kerb stones define a former peat stand, of a type common on the hills above Dinas Mawddwy (Gwynedd).

Peat house on the hills above the Conwy Valley (Conwy).

roofs. Two peat houses on the uplands above Rowen in the Conwy Valley stand above damp, boggy ground (SH 7334 7357 and SH 7391 7346). One of them shows three phases of construction, the earliest probably of the eighteenth century. The roof is constructed of layers of slabs, or corbels, over which there may have been a turf covering. The inside is cramped and airless, but at least protected from the rain. Working on the exposed hills for long periods encouraged the building of shelters, or even squatting in abandoned cottages, both of which have been described elsewhere.

SLATE QUARRIES AND MINES

There is a rich heritage of slate quarrying in Wales and the lion's share of it is found in the unenclosed uplands. Slate quarrying is not confined to the north-west of Wales. The slate roofs of Pembrokeshire were derived from the Preseli Hills, where the largest quarry was at Rosebush. In north-east Wales, slate was sourced from around Llangollen in Denbighshire, and there were large slate quarries at Llangynog in the Tanat Valley in Powys.

Remains of a peat house on the hills above the Conwy Valley (Conwy).

Slate is a sedimentary rock that has been metamorphosed by compression and heat, both a result of tectonic activity. It is usually described as being found in veins. The orientation of these veins varies, which in turn influences when and how it has been exploited. The thin layers make it easy to split, making it ideal for use on roofs, but for many centuries it was a local building material put to all sorts of uses, including slabs for walls and thick graded slates for roofs – towns like Caernarfon have plenty of surviving examples of this. Compared to traditional roofing materials, such as thatch, thin roofing slates proved to be a relatively lightweight and durable material and so were one of the earliest quarry materials from Wales to find a national and international market. Slate became one of the universal building materials that made the Victorian building boom so successful.

The earliest archaeological evidence for slate quarrying comes in the Roman period, when slates and slabs were used in buildings at Segontium fort near Caernarfon. Evidence of early slate quarrying can be found in the hills, although there is usually no evidence that tells you whether it was worked in the thirteenth or the eighteenth century.

Early slate workings near Llan Ffestiniog (Gwynedd) are small in scale, with no associated transport infrastructure.

As a general rule, the smaller the scale of works, the older it is likely to be. The early quarries will have only minimal spoil tips, no or minimal evidence of dressing the stone on site, and none of the obvious signs of a bespoke transport infrastructure that is an integral part of the large nineteenth-century works. It is also worth remembering, however, that many early workings could have been destroyed by the industrial-scale quarrying of the nineteenth century.

Medieval workings comprised mainly a series of pits, a practice that continued into the eighteenth century at Cilgwyn (Caernarfonshire), where early pits have now been infilled. Early small-scale pits for slate are likely to be found on the lower rather than the high ground, as close to settlements as was convenient. A survey of Y Cefn (SH 7088 4160), near Llan Ffestiniog, found over 70 quarry pits, which provided building stone and roofing materials for the nearby town, probably worked by local men exercising their right of access to the mountain land. Although many small quarries are likely to belong to the seventeenth and eighteenth centuries, periods for which there are surviving local buildings, some of them may well be earlier. Evidence of pre-industrial quarries can also be found on the original one-inch Ordnance Survey maps compiled in the early-nineteenth century. A good example is at Penantigi Uchaf (SH 8067 1576) on the hills east of Dolgellau, which consists of no more than a sheer quarry face about 8m high and a mound of spoil. Similar to this is a small quarry near Corris at Mynydd y Waun (SH 7629 1324), a quarry face 10m high and overgrown quarry floor.

The capitalist phase of slate extraction began in the late eighteenth century. Richard Pennant (1737–1808), who became the first Lord Penrhyn and who had amassed a fortune in the slave trade, established a link to the coast for the export of roof slates and capitalised the industry, a process that turned independent quarrymen into waged labour. Other landowners, notably the Assheton-Smith family, who founded the Dinorwic quarry, followed suit. The industry expanded rapidly in the nineteenth century as new transport infrastructure facilitated the export market, peaking in the 1870s, before a slow decline set in, brought about by competition from imported slates and the expansion of the tile industry.

Techniques for large-scale mining in the capitalist phase depended upon the local geology. In the Ffestiniog area the veins dip sharply at a steep angle, so it was not possible to work it from the surface. The underground workings in the locality are nevertheless conventionally referred to as quarries. Suitable veins of rock were discovered, to some extent, by trial and error. Exploratory levels were driven through hard, commercially useless rock in search of suitable slate. In the field this means that the spoil tips and the rock types of these trials will not contain any slate. They can easily be mistaken for metal prospecting.

Slate could not be quarried in the same way as hard rock because of its tendency to shatter. This limited the height of the quarry faces to about 20m maximum. Many small quarries were worked as single faces, but in the larger quarries the rock was won in a series of benched galleries, leaving behind a terraced slope with vertical or steep quarry

The large quarry pit at Minllyn Quarry, near Dinas Mawddwy (Gwynedd), has slowly reverted back to nature.

faces and level working floors. This open-sided arrangement is best seen in the Penrhyn and Dinorwic quarries in Eryri, and Rosebush in Pembrokeshire. An alternative was to work the quarry as a single pit, which is deeper than the surrounding topography. To do this the quarry floor had to be lowered progressively, and, when the quarry was situated on a valley side, tunnels were made through the hillside to reach it. These kinds of workings are common throughout the North Wales region.

Only about 10 per cent of the stone removed from a quarry formed part of the final product. The remainder was waste, and was dumped close to the quarry. Enormous spoil tips are one of the characteristic features of slate quarries and are among the most conspicuous features to be found in the quarrying landscape. Abandoned quarries or underground chambers could be used for backfilling with waste; but, in practice, there was far too much spoil to do anything other than pile it up on the surface. From the early nineteenth century, it was tipped from simple railway wagons, on lines that were extended as the tip lengthened. The tips evolved into the shape of long embankments,

Large quarry finger tips at Rhiwbach Quarry near Cwm Penmachno (Conwy).

known as finger tips, often bunched together in the form of several fingers, creating several conjoined embankments. Some of them were so large that they had to be carefully managed by means of retaining walls and the incorporation of carefully constructed conduits to allow the uninterrupted flow of natural streams.

Spoil tips became quarries in their own right during hard times. You can see evidence of this in the form of irregularities in the profile of a tip, or more obviously where there is evidence of crudely-built shelters. These were built by the workmen and were occupied by men splitting and trimming the slates on site.

Once the slate was quarried, it had to be processed. The quarries produced a variety of products. Roofing material was the principal one, but slabs were also produced for use such as cold shelves in pantries, writing slates used in schools, gravestones, fireplaces, urinals and billiard tables, among several others. The slate was processed on site and evidence of how this was done can be seen at slate quarries of the nineteenth century and later.

The splitting of slate for roof material was never fully mechanised, though, in the late-nineteenth century, mills were developed that cut the slate into raw blocks that were then split by hand, and trimmed by guillotine or a rotating blade. Hand-splitting of slate was done in three-sided cabins known as *gwaliau* (*gwal* means literally a lair). The fact that one of the sides was open helps to identify the presence of these structures long after the roofs have collapsed and the walls have been reduced in height. Most were built of slate rubble and had mono-pitch roofs. Penrhyn quarry had several hundred of them, mostly now demolished, but they are a common sight at old slate quarries, often built in rows and with an adjacent level area that was used as a stack-yard. In these simple shelters the slate was trimmed and split, to make roof slates, without any mechanical aids. The shelters sometimes built on spoil tips, described above, were similar in form.

Remains of a three-sided iron wagon which was used to transport slate waste to the tips.

The main mill at Rhos slate quarry (Conwy) is now roofless but the long line of *gwaliau* is clearly visible.

Mechanical processing was carried out in slate mills, which are the largest structures found at quarry sites. Mills are typically long single-storey buildings, although the most famous of the slate mills, at Ynys y Pandy near Porthmadog (SH 5499 4336), is a notable exception in being multi-storey, as well as being sited some way below the Gorsedda Quarry it served, which is up on the high ground above Llyn Ystradllyn reservoir. Although the mills could sometimes assist in manufacturing roofing slates, they were generally engaged in other, larger work. Whereas the *gwal* was a place of hand-crafting, the mill was a factory, and consequently a much more regulated place.

Power in the nineteenth century was generally from waterwheels, which replaced the hand-operated saws that had been used from the seventeenth century. Later on, steam engines, water turbines, internal

The upper reservoir at Bwlch Camllan (Gwynedd) has a dam wall constructed of outer stone faces with a rougher inner core, grassed over in this example.

combustion engines, compressed air and electricity superseded them. Mills operated on simple, basic principles, even if the layout of mills varied considerably. They relied on tramways to transport the bulky materials. Slate blocks were delivered at one end, while the waste and the finished slates or slabs were dispatched from one or more openings at the other end. Nearly all of the mills were built using material to hand, which usually meant waste slate, and had multiple entrances and exits.

Water power systems are recognisable as much for the wider infrastructure as the relatively plain narrow wheelpits. Water may have been abundant on the hills but it still needed managing to ensure a constant supply, especially in a landscape overcrowded with enterprises all competing for water from the same gathering grounds. Waterwheels were supplied from ponds fed by watercourses, just as they were in other industries. Reservoirs were constructed, and in North Wales the dams were built with stone walls to the inner and outer faces, with a rougher core between them, which is a distinct regional characteristic that makes them easy to identify. The place to look for a waterwheel pit is in the centre or against one of the walls of the mill. The wheelpits were substantially-built with large blocks, and may retain the bearing blocks in the centre where the wheel was mounted. Characteristic features inside the pit are scratch marks made by the wheel as it turned, and an outlet, or tail race, at the downstream end. Waterwheels were the preferred source of power throughout the nineteenth century, for the same reason that they were employed in other, especially remote, industries. The Welsh hills could supply plenty of water, and wheels were cheap, simple to maintain and could provide plenty of power.

Waterwheels were built of cast iron, but do not expect to find an intact example at a surviving slate mill – a fine specimen can be seen at the National Slate Museum. Once their working lives had ceased, the wheels were removed for their scrap value or else sold to be used elsewhere. Other forms of power have likewise left little evidence behind.

Despite the loss of its timber elements, the wheelpit at Rhos slate quarry (Conwy) and the line of pillars that supported the water launder, show how water power was utilised.

Steam engines were valuable plant that could also be sold on for use elsewhere, or else for scrap. Wrought-iron boilers also had a scrap value that made them worth removing from sites. However, the engine bases are often identifiable by holding-down bolts spread out on levelled ground, and by the bases of boilers and an adjoining chimney. Old stacks at slate works were usually square in plan at the base, and were placed outside of mill buildings, for obvious reasons.

In addition to the processing mills, power was also employed in the drainage of underground workings, raising materials from underground

The engine house and boiler stack at Rhiwbach Quarry, above Penmachno (Conwy), was used to wind materials up a shaft on the far side of the building.

and raising and lowering slate or waste at inclined planes, as well as for transporting materials by means of aerial ropeways, known as *blondins* after their French inventor. Inclined planes are a common sight in the slate landscapes of North Wales.

The bigger the quarry, the more extensive its ancillary buildings are likely to be. The most common of these buildings are smithies, used for sharpening tools and general maintenance. Look for evidence of a hearth and chimney, and a trough for quenching. Nettles often grow where clinker has been spread. Next to a smithy might be a joiners' shop, an engineering workshop and perhaps a stores. Only the larger quarries had offices. The scaling-up of the industry in the nineteenth century required accurate means of measuring output. The simplest means is the weighbridge and weighbridge house. The weighbridge is usually recognisable because it is on the line of a tramroad, and has a pit for the counterweight. Next to it, the weighbridge house may be a simple structure of one room, but with a fireplace. Gunpowder was used in slate extraction from the nineteenth century and has left distinctive buildings. Magazines for storing explosives were sited away from

A weighbridge house, with pit for the counterweight,
at Drum Quarry near Llan Ffestiniog (Gwynedd).

the main works, and feature baffle walls and heavy slab roofs. At the quarry itself the workmen had their own shelters for protection during blasting, known as a *cwt mochel ffeiar*, a simple windowless structure in which the entrance looks away from the quarry face.

The remote location of many slate quarries made it difficult for workmen to return home of an evening. The answer to this was to house the men in barracks, where they lived during the week, returning home at weekends. Barracks were a product of the massive expansion of the slate industry in the latter half of the nineteenth century, although they were built at other remotely-sited industries too, like lead and copper mines. The Anglesey Barracks at Dinorwic (SH 5895 6023) is the most photogenic of these, but it is relatively close to Llanberis and therefore in a reasonably convenient location. Others are found in high and remote places that were challenging in winter, even setting aside the spartan conditions inside. Mostly, barracks were inhabited

Anglesey Barracks, below Dinorwic Quarry (Gwynedd).

Remains of a magazine at Drum Quarry (Gwynedd).

by the workmen only. Occasionally, men brought their families with them, but these would be the barracks near villages and shops. The ones you encounter in the remote uplands are most likely to have been the more rudimentary kind, recognisable as a long and narrow block, invariably built from waste material at the quarry.

It is difficult to pick the 'best' slate-quarrying sites because there are so many criteria that make slate quarries worth visiting. Sometimes it is the survival of their archaeology, and sometimes it can simply be the sheer remoteness of the site. Some were larger, employed more people and have more spectacular remains than others. Dinorwic Quarry, which is also home to the National Slate Museum, is perhaps the prime example, but out on the hills it is usually the smaller quarries that are encountered by accident.

The archaeology of Minllyn Quarry (SH 851 139), close to Dinas Mawddwy, extends from the steep forested slopes above the A470 out on to the open hillside, beyond which is the remains of an incline linking it to Cae Abaty, an earlier and more remote slate quarry. Owned by the Carlyle Slate and Slab Company, Minllyn enjoyed a period of success from the 1870s until its closure in 1925. It was described by the *Carnarvon and Denbigh Herald* in 1873, when it gave employment to 60 men:

> as a slab quarry it is one of the most important in the country. The blocks can be literally obtained in any required size. The plan of the quarry is the usual system of underground chambers – the uppermost chamber being uncovered. The blocks are conveyed down inclines to a large machine room at the foot of the hill, where there are over forty planing and sawing machines driven by water power.

Much of this remains visible at the site today. The slate was quarried from a deep pit, requiring tunnels to remove the material to the appropriate inclined plane, superseding the earlier underground workings that can be identified by the presence of spoil tips. The incline conveyed the slate to the processing mill, built in 1845 – a now roofless building where the workflow is clearly discernible with its uphill and downhill ends. No evidence of the waterwheel is now visible, except for a pond high on the hill above the quarry, but there is tell-tale evidence of a later steam engine in the form of a boiler stack and a cast-iron pipe that delivered water to the boilers. A very steep incline descends through forestry to a former storehouse and rail yard in the valley, to the quarrymen's settlement of Minllyn, where the houses were far superior to the traditional rudimentary cottages.

Gorsedda Quarry (SH 572 452) is in the Glaslyn district of Eryri, on the uplands north of Porthmadog. It is a landscape with extensive remains, even though it was not one of the more successful slate-quarrying enterprises of the nineteenth century. Although there was slate quarrying here early in the nineteenth century, what you see on the site is the result of little over a decade of working, which began in 1854 when the quarry was developed by the Bavarian mining engineer Henry Tobias Tschudy von Ulster. The visible remains are of large terraces, or benched

The barracks at Rhosydd Quarry (Gwynedd).

The mill at Minllyn Quarry, above Dinas Mawddwy (Gwynedd). On the left is the boiler
stack belonging to the mill steam engine.

galleries, on the hillside – very impressive for a quarry with such a short life and served by a central inclined plane, with associated spoil tips and remains of a railway from where the slate was transported to Ynys y Pandy slab mill, and thence to Porthmadog. Aside from the typical *gwaliau* and blast shelters, there is also the remains of a small, permanent settlement, known as Treforys, which has already been described.

At Cwmorthin is one of the larger, and most interesting, quarry complexes in the Ffestiniog district. The main developments at Cwmorthin Quarry (SH 680 460) began in the 1860s, but there had been half a century of quarrying at the site by then. The most extensive workings were underground, but on the surface are the remains of three processing mills with associated transport systems, including inclined planes, plus smaller ancillary features like a magazine, a row of cottages, office and the site of an old chapel. Uphill from Cwmorthin are other quarries, giving a good impression of how crowded the landscape was with competing interests in the slate industry. Beyond the upper end of Llyn

Benched galleries, with accompanying spoil tips, are well preserved at Gorsedda Quarry (Gwynedd).

This half-tunnel was built to prevent spoil from falling on to the railway between
Gorsedda Quarry (Gwynedd) and the mill at Ynys y Pandy, about four miles away.

Conglog Slate Quarry above Llyn Cwmorthin (Gwynedd). The mill and the line
of pillars carrying the water launder to the water wheel are clearly visible.

Cwmorthin, the Conglog quarry (SH 6692 4656) was also worked by
successive companies in the second half of the nineteenth century. The
remains of this include the pits that led to underground levels, and a
large slate mill on the lower part of the site. The mill was water-powered and one of the conspicuous features of the site is a line of stone pillars on which the water launder feeding the waterwheel was carried. A
track leads uphill from Conglog to another large quarry, Rhosydd (SH
6654 4623), and the smaller Croesor Quarry (SH 6575 4570), where slate
was worked from underground. Rhosydd is a long straggling hilltop site
which was expanded in the 1850s, where the slate was quarried from two
deep pits that had to be drained using adits. The archaeological remains
on the site include those of water-powered mills (albeit largely taken
down), inclined planes and a large barrack block at 450m above sea level.
Tramways from Rhosydd and Croesor led to steep inclined planes, by
which means slate was transported westwards into the deep valley of
Cwm Croesor. The head of the incline offers one of the most magnifi-
cent views to be had in North Wales.

Metal mining

Lead, copper, manganese, silver, zinc and gold have all been mined from the Welsh hills. Often these non-ferrous metals are found in close proximity – significant deposits of silver are a common by-product of lead mines, for example. It means that some mines began digging for one mineral and ended up mining another, like the Red Dragon mine (SH 8364 1390) near Dinas Mawddwy, which began mining lead in 1852 but became a gold mine after black gossan was found there in 1854. The other metal found in the Welsh hills is iron; however, as it is generally found in different parts of Wales, was treated differently on site and was a major international (let alone Welsh) industry, it is described separately.

Copper was the first metal to be exploited from the Welsh hills. Mining at Copa Hill, Cwmystwyth, has been radiocarbon dated to about 2100BC, although it may have begun earlier, and it continued until about 1600BC, by which time the easily-worked deposits had been exhausted. At Nant-yr-Eira, on the eastern side of Plynlimon (SN 826 874), charcoal samples have established that copper mining was in operation in the Late Bronze Age, although in historic times the mine was worked extensively for lead. Copper was the chief component of bronze (with tin) and, later, brass (with zinc). Copper mining was otherwise concentrated in Eryri, with other important centres of production on the Great Orme and Parys Mountain on Anglesey. There was a boom in demand for copper wire in the electricity era that began in the late-nineteenth century, but it was a time when Welsh mines could no longer compete profitably with foreign sources, or even meet demand, so this was when the native industry declined.

In Roman times Wales was one of the principal sources of lead in Britain. Lead was a versatile metal capable of many applications, including water pipes, coffins, toys and as a component of pewter (an alloy comprising about 70% tin and 30% lead). A malleable, easily-worked metal, lead was used as a roofing material in medieval Britain, and was used in the manufacture of glass, while muskets fired lead shot. During the medieval period extraction of lead ore therefore thrived, and the huge monastic estates of Strata Marcella and Strata Florida in mid Wales invested in its development, including the extensive mines at Cwm Ystwyth. Many of these mines fell into disuse a century after the Dissolution of the monasteries, when the monastic estate passed to the Crown, but were revived in the 1630s after Thomas Bushell (1594–1674) was granted the royal mines of Ceredigion by Charles I. Bushell managed to recover old mines that had flooded, including some apparently of Roman date, and pioneered the use of adits rather than shafts to exploit veins of ore from underground (some of these mines would be classified as lowland sites according to our criteria).

By the eighteenth century Britain was Europe's leading producer of lead. But the heyday of the Welsh metal mines was to come in the nineteenth century, when demand for minerals was a direct consequence of the industrial revolution, and before competition from foreign ore-fields priced the Welsh mines out of the market. The majority of metal mines were exploiting lead and zinc. Zinc was used in brass manufacture, and in the nineteenth century was used to galvanise iron, helping it to resist corrosion. The most well-known example of this is probably corrugated iron used as a roofing material (often known informally as zinc roofing).

Silver was also obtained from the lead-ore fields in Ceredigion, in certain parts of Powys, such as Llangynog, and in north-east Wales, notably on Halkyn Mountain. It has made a greater contribution to the Welsh economy than gold. Thomas Bushell succeeded in extracting silver from his lead mines in Ceredigion, which were productive enough for a royal mint to have been designated at Aberystwyth Castle in 1637 for striking coins from Welsh silver. Manganese, which was used to enhance the strengths of certain grades of steel, had an even smaller geographical range – around the Arenig mountains and on the Llŷn Peninsula.

Gold was first worked probably in Roman times, when there were extensive mines at Dolaucothi in Carmarthenshire; however, evidence of gold mining in the uplands is almost invariably associated with the mid-nineteenth-century mining boom. The principal area of production was the 'Dolgellau Gold-belt', roughly from Barmouth to Trawsfynydd.

There was also extensive prospecting in the Clwydian Hills, although without any commercial production, or even definitive evidence that gold was actually present. Evidence of upland gold workings is therefore mostly confined to small-scale prospecting – the general rule with gold mines is that more gold went into them than ever came out of them. Other minerals have been successfully exploited, but only on a very small scale – barytes, calcite, cobalt, arsenic and antimony.

The non-ferrous metal mines of Wales are found mainly in mid and North Wales. Although it was primarily an upland industry carried out often in remote places, invariably the most accessible reserves were exploited first, which were often from lowland sites like the Dolaucothi gold mines and Goginon silver mines. Upland sites, with little or no existing transport infrastructure, made it difficult to establish and sustain profitable mining businesses. The metal mines of eighteenth- and nineteenth-century Wales are to some extent a triumph of hope over experience – with a pattern of initial investment, some modest success, followed by failure, and then a new injection of capital by a different owner. The mines, run by managers known as mine captains, were worked on leasehold arrangements as landowners were keen to retain their mineral rights, and the potential riches they offered.

Like quarries, upland metal mines differ in scale, and the remains left behind are varied, encompassing surface workings, entrances to underground workings, building remains associated with ore-processing and remains of water-supply systems. Early mines are not rich in artefacts and so are notoriously difficult to date. Many of them have evidently been destroyed by later workings. The earliest must have been surface workings, which is how the presence of mineral deposits was first recognised. When ore was dug from the surface it was often aided by a method of removing the top soil known as hushing – a process used by the Romans as well as during the medieval period. The concept was simple: to store a large volume of water which was released suddenly, creating a torrent that washed away all of the loose ground overlying the bedrock. The technique continued to be used occasionally in the eighteenth century. Perhaps the best example in Wales is at Craig y Mwyn,

One of the breached hushing tanks at Craig y Mwyn lead mines (Powys), beside a track.
Water was released from here to the hillside below on the left.

A view looking downhill at Craig y Mwyn surface workings (Powys), where
the direction of watercourses and hushing channels are clearly visible.

near Pistyll Rhaeadr waterfall, where there was mining from Roman times until the nineteenth century (SJ 074 285). The steep hillside is a landscape of banks, pits and troughs all derived from the flow of water and digging out of ore. Leats gathered water from the hillside above and channelled it into reservoirs, or 'miners pools'. Only so much can be exploited in this way, however. In 1747 the mining agent of the Powys Estates sunk a shaft, which is easily located at the top of the hill, away from the opencast workings (SJ 0741 2833). There are other significant remains of hushing at the medieval lead mines on Copa Hill (SN 811 752) near Cwmystwyth, and at Pen Dylife (SN 849 933) by the upper reaches of the Clywedog river above Llanidloes.

Metal was also won underground from both shafts and adits. The latter are near-horizontal tunnels (in practice with a slight uphill gradient to allow them to drain naturally) driven into the sides of hills to exploit specific seams. Shafts are vertical and required some mechanical means of raising ore to the surface. For safety reasons, they have usually been plugged and are often fenced off. It is not advisable to test how deep they are. Likewise, adits are generally at least partially blocked, and accessible only by the more determined cavers.

The shaft sunk at Craig Mwyn lead mines (Powys) in 1747.

Areas of metal mining have other characteristic features. The most numerous are trial mines, which can be in the form of prospecting trenches and short adits. The adits often look very promising from the outside but once you look into them and see that they are only 5–10m long, it is obvious that they were only trials. The trenches are much more numerous and can be as little as 1m wide, extending for about 5–10m in length. It is not possible to tell which minerals were prospected in these trials. In fairness, even the prospectors themselves did not always know, and occasionally found deposits they didn't expect. In 1770 Elizabeth Baker began prospecting at Tyllau Mwn, on the remote moorland north of Dinas Mawddwy: 'We have sunk a shaft five yards, the vein is about four feet wide … I hope to God it may prove a copper mine tho' the magnet acts powerfully upon what is raisd'. Plans for a copper mine turned into an ironstone mine.

Non-ferrous ores have a relatively low metal content compared to iron ores (for example the yield of copper from copper ore is less than 1 per cent), so there was often an initial processing conducted at the mine itself. In the medieval period this included smelting of lead ore in boles. These were hearths dug into the ground on slopes, in which lead ore was smelted using charcoal, aided by an updraft of air to bring the ore to a high-enough temperature to extract the lead. Evidence for smelting has been discovered at Copa Hill near Cwmystwyth, and John Leland made a passing reference to the environmental damage done by local lead smelting when he visited the area in 1535. Archaeological remains of copper smelting are signalled by the discovery of burnt stone fragments on the ground, but the process has not left any visible features in the landscape. The non-ferrous mining of the

Trial pits, like this shallow elongated depression near Dylife (Powys), are common in the metal-mining regions.

TOP: Trial adit in the Dyfngwm mining landscape (Powys); ABOVE LEFT: A trial mine on the hill above Llyn Cregennan in Eryri (Gwynedd), a familiar sight in the uplands; ABOVE RIGHT: The adit at Dyfngwm lead mine (Powys) was worked in the nineteenth century and again in the 1930s.

eighteenth century and later is more conspicuous, since the larger scale of working in this period required substantial structures for the processing (not smelting) of ores on site. This took the form of crushing and washing the ores to reduce the amount of waste material, which was important when transporting a very bulky product by packhorse or road.

Power was used at the mines for raising ores to the surface, drainage of underground workings (rare in Wales) and the processing of ores. In later years, steam and diesel engines were used to provide the motive power for the crushers, but for most of the mines which had processing facilities, water power was the preferred and cheapest option. The problem with steam was the need to transport coal, a heavy and bulky fuel, to remote landscapes where there was no rail infrastructure. There was less competition over the water-gathering grounds of ore-mines than there was in the crowded slate-industry landscapes, and the leats can extend over long distances on the hillside, where they may easily be mistaken for paths, except that they follow the contours of the hill, allowing only for a gentle gradient.

Dressing of ores usually involved crushing, washing, then separating off the small pieces that were metal rich. Non-ferrous ores emerged from the mine in lumps of various sizes, which had to be 'dressed' on site in order that ore with a high metal content could be shipped. Firstly the lumps were broken down with hammers, often manually, into pieces small enough to be passed under ore crushers. Mechanised ore crushers reduced the lumps of rock further into small particles, small enough to be passed through a mesh. Jiggers shook the ore so that the heavier, metal-rich pieces collected at the bottom. Crushed ore was also washed by allowing water to flow over it in a round pit known as a buddle. It was then allowed to settle, which allowed the lighter, non-metallic pieces of rock to float to the surface where they could be skimmed off. The machinery for these processes very rarely survives. Most of it was made of wood and has rotted. Otherwise, plant was sold off when a mine was closed. The dressing process produced large amounts of waste, so spoil tips are a common feature of these sites (although spoil was often used to backfill disused shafts).

Part of the rock-cut leat that fed the waterwheel at Castle Rock mine (Powys) on the banks of the Clywedog.

Metal mines also have ancillary buildings like a smithy, perhaps an office and a shelter for workmen, and often a magazine for storing gunpowder. The latter are small, windowless structures that can usually be identified because they are placed well away from the main workings.

Mining sites are fascinating in their own right, usually giving a sense of the isolation experienced by the men who worked in them. But which of the non-ferrous mining sites are worth making a conscious effort to go and see? A good place to start is the former metal mines that have been restored and are open to the public, such as Bryntail Lead Mine (below Llyn Clywedog near Llanidloes), Minera Lead Mine (near Wrexham), Sygun Copper Mine (near Beddgelert) and Silver Mountain (near Ponterwyd on the A44). These are well interpreted remains, with restored machinery in some instances, which can help to make sense of the unrestored mining remains on the remote hillsides.

Cwmystwyth mines (SN 803 746), spread out on either side of the Ystwyth Valley, through which runs the Aberystwyth mountain road, show many of the characteristic features of non-ferrous mining in the uplands, principally of copper in prehistory and lead in historic times. They are especially worth visiting because the remains cover a very long time period, and because they are relatively accessible from the road, although to see the earlier remains requires a steep uphill walk. Here, the recovery of some artefacts suggests prehistoric working, and, as part of the estate of Strata Florida

This isolated structure was a magazine serving the former South Cambrian Lead Mine, now submerged beneath Nant y Moch reservoir (Powys).

The foundations of a large processing mill built *c.*1900, originally roofed, dominate the surviving mining landscape of Cwmystwyth (Ceredigion).

Abbey, there was work here in medieval times too. From the seventeenth to the early-twentieth century, mining here continued sporadically, under various owners who tended to invest heavily, sometimes making a profit, before their businesses failed and another owner took up the baton, sometimes following a period of abandonment.

The remains that can be seen today are dominated by the foundations of the large processing mill, built *c.*1900, which was originally powered by a water turbine. This whole area is now open to the sky but was once covered by a large corrugated-iron shed. Other buildings near the road include a crusher house and offices. On the south side of the valley, the steep sides have adits, associated spoil tips and evidence of ore chutes and tramways, as well as the paths taken by workmen to their workplace, much of which can be seen from the mountain road.

Some of the most intensively mined landscapes in Wales are to be found on Halkyn Mountain in Flintshire. Galena (lead sulphide) and sphalerite (zinc sulphide) were the main metals mined, but silver and copper have also been mined here and there are other quarries for limestone and clay. The scale of mining increased in the nineteenth century, including water and steam-powered processing and drainage structures, but a policy of clearing derelict buildings has meant that few of them have survived, and the story of mining here is told largely through the earthworks of abandoned workings. Here, the earliest lead workings can be identified as lines of pits that followed a vein of ore. Some of them might be prehistoric, Roman or medieval, but most belong to the seventeenth century when small plots of land were leased annually, essentially a length of about 30 yards known as a meer (the customary term for a measure of land derived from Derbyshire lead mining). Some of the unworked boundary stones that defined these meers have survived, all about 1m tall.

The mines take the form of shallow pits from which the ore was raised by a hand-operated windlass, or by use of a horse whim. Today they survive as pits with rings of spoil around them – the extent of the spoil mounds giving some indication of the original depths of the pits. As with other areas of intensive mining, there are also numerous trial pits, as well as some deeper shafts – the deepest of which have all been capped

Two groups of ruined cottages stand next to an abandoned level near Cwmystwyth (Ceredigion).

The hillside above the Yswyth near Cwmystwyth (Ceredigion) is a rich mining landscape of miners' paths, tramways, old levels and spoil tips.

by pyramids of rubble stone, or are fenced off. Some of the numerous tracks on the common land were once tramways; although, because they were only small-scale operations, packhorse or horse and cart were probably the usual method of transporting the ore. Ore may once have been smelted on the mountain itself, which is indicated by the place-name element 'ball' in Pen-y-*Ball* and Coita *Ball* – a corruption of 'bole'. It is a good example of how maps can reveal aspects of history that cannot be seen on the ground, however sharp your focus is.

Dylife was a very small mining settlement – although big enough for a church, three chapels and a school in the late-nineteenth century – that served extensive mining operations across an area southwards to the upper reaches of the Clywedog river in Powys. There could have been Roman mining here, since there is a small fortlet at nearby Penycrocbren (SN 8560 9348), but no datable evidence is visible on the ground. Most of the mining evidence dates from the seventeenth to the twentieth centuries. Thomas Bushell leased the mineral rights here

A landscape of old shafts and bellpits are the remains of early lead
working on Halkyn Mountain (Flintshire).

A typical bell pit on Halkyn Mountain (Flintshire).

in 1640 but by 1700 the historical sources refer only to underground workings, so the considerable evidence of surface workings must be older than that. There are numerous hushing channels, with associated ponds and small trial workings, lining the Pen Dylife ridge on the south side of the road.

The later workings at Dylife are closer to the river. The evidence includes adits, and the remains of a large water-powered crusher mill fed by a very long leat alongside the river. By 1901 the works had been abandoned, but it opened again for four years from 1931 – a period that has left an even bigger imprint in the landscape, in the form of large concrete processing mills and sludge tanks beside the river. Waste from ore processing was allowed to settle in these tanks, enabling any residual ore to separate from the remainder.

Remains of the 1930s processing mill at Dyfngwm Mine on the banks of the Clywedog (Powys). In the twentieth century, concrete replaced masonry for many industrial structures.

Earthwork remains of a large sludge tank on the banks of the Clywedog at Dyfngwm.

IRONSTONE MINING AND WORKING

Iron is the most common metal in the natural world and it was exploited in Wales with far greater commercial success, and on a far larger scale, than any other metal. In the first half of the nineteenth century, Wales was the leading centre of iron production in Britain, but the industry had evolved rapidly in the eighteenth century when coke replaced charcoal as the fuel for smelting, and continued into the twentieth century and the age of steel. The chief area of production was the South Wales Coalfield, but there was a significant centre of ironworking in the Denbighshire coalfield in north-east Wales. None of that means that the iron industry has left more archaeological evidence in the uplands than other metals, however. A general rule of industrial archaeology is that as the scale of operations increased, so does the likelihood that the evidence has been entirely cleared away after abandonment. The iron industry is a good example of this. Surface working of iron ore at the edge of the South Wales Coalfield, roughly at the boundary of the

Bannau Brycheiniog National Park and astride the A465 Heads of the Valleys road, had an enormous impact on the natural landscape, but these remains have survived poorly compared to the slate landscapes of North Wales, for two related reasons. Firstly, much of it was destroyed by large-scale open-cast working in the twentieth century, using large mechanical diggers; and secondly, because post-industrial landscapes were considered to be eyesores, large areas of industrial landscape have been regraded, erasing their history.

The iron ore was traditionally smelted close to the place where it was mined. In the Industrial Revolution of the eighteenth and nineteenth centuries, that meant in the river valleys of South Wales, with a concentration near the heads of the valleys. Before that, there were furnaces in the uplands of Wales, although they are very difficult to identify.

Although it is much more commonly found than other metals, iron is very difficult to work, which explains why we had a Bronze Age before an Iron Age. In Britain the Iron Age is a period in which archaeologists almost never find any iron, with some exceptions – one of the most spectacular of Iron Age discoveries in Wales was the hoard of metalware from Llyn Fawr, the glacial cwm just beyond the head of the Rhondda Valley, which included bronze cauldrons and axes, and an iron sword and sickles. The material did not become widespread until the Roman period, although the Roman iron industry in Britain was centred not in Wales, but in the Kent and Sussex Weald.

The earliest ironworks exploited the ores easiest to extract, which in upland Wales is known as bog iron ore, formed when iron-bearing waters meet organic material and the iron coalesces beneath the moorland turf. One of these sources was in the Gamallt Valley near Llan Ffestiniog, but there is no visible trace of any mining activity there now. Fortunately, we know about it because evidence of the accompanying nearby smelting operations has survived. At Bryn y Castell (SH 7281 4297), where iron was smelted over two periods between about 100BC and AD 250, there is evidence of smelting and smithing in a large hut circle within a hillfort.

Evidence of early ironworking in the uplands is confined to smelting rather than mining, but from the medieval period that is reversed – the furnaces are built in the lowlands and coastal locations, and upland landscapes provide evidence of exploitation and transportation of iron ore. There are only small areas where iron ore could be mined outside of the coalfields. The Tir Stent mines, near to the Cross Foxes public house on the A470 road to Dolgellau, supplied the Brymbo Ironworks near Wrexham in the early-twentieth century, and may have previously sent ore to the Dolgun blast furnace at nearby Brithdir in the eighteenth century. The site is within forestry, but there are more remote ironstone workings at Tyllau Mwn, described above, which also supplied the ironworks of north-east Wales in the nineteenth century.

However, in Wales, the copious reserves of iron ore were found in the coalfields, and the iron industry in Wales developed rapidly from the mid-eighteenth century when the coal and iron industries became combined. This was established largely at the Cyfarthfa, Dowlais and Plymouth Works in Merthyr Tydfil. It suddenly made large-scale investment in the iron industry very attractive, both to entrepreneurs and especially to landowners who owned large areas of what had hitherto been economically unprofitable upland valleys and moors. In 1790 William Lewis claimed that the Dowlais company would have to build six new blast furnaces in order to meet demand. In 1788 Lord Abergavenny leased the mineral rights of a large estate, covering a 12,000-acre tract of land in northern Monmouthshire; so large that, after the Blaenavon Ironworks was established there in 1789, there were sufficient raw materials to establish a separate works at Nantyglo in 1792. Blaenavon and Nantyglo were among the new type of integrated ironworks, established from the 1760s at Merthyr Tydfil, where the whole process of iron manufacture was carried out – the smelting of iron ore to produce pig iron and the further refining to produce wrought iron, known in the trade as bar iron.

The demographic, economic and political geography of Wales was transformed by the rise of the South Wales Coalfield. Its success was built on the ease with which its mineral wealth could be exploited.

The Roman camp at Bryn y Castell, near Llan Ffestiniog (Gwynedd), was a site of upland iron smelting in the second and third centuries.

The geology of the South Wales Coalfield is of inclined beds which break surface at the heads of the valleys, and then become deeper to the south towards the coast. Coal and iron ore could therefore be dug from the surface and from shallow workings. Like other industries, large quantities of water were needed as a source of power, which were channelled from extensive gathering grounds on the hills.

The hills around Merthyr Tydfil once boasted the most extensive mining remains of the Industrial Revolution period. Its two largest ironworks, at Cyfarthfa and Dowlais, were Britain's largest works in the first half of the nineteenth century. On the east side of the town, where the Dowlais and the smaller Penydarren Ironworks exploited the rich mineral reserves, extensive twentieth-century opencast workings have reduced a large area of landscape to year zero. However, even here there are islands of untouched industrial archaeology, as there are on the west side of the town, above the A470 bypass, on a hillside exploited from 1765 to supply the Cyfarthfa Ironworks. Of the latter there are even vestigial remains of a short canal which carried coal and iron ore to the works (SO 0425 0544).

Intensive exploitation of iron ore over a century, and subsequent large-scale opencast mining, have meant that evidence of early extraction is only rarely identifiable. Although veins containing ironstone were dug from underground (properly termed 'mines', as opposed to 'collieries' where coal was dug), in practice the evidence of ironstone mining you are likely to encounter on the hills is from opencast workings. In many places it was simply dug from the surface, leaving pits known as patches, but the greatest impact on the landscape was made by the crude processing of the ore in a technique known as 'scouring'. The practice of hushing has already been described, whereby water was impounded and then released to remove the overburden covering the mineral veins. Hushing was sometimes used in the extraction of ironstone. Scouring is different, however, as it is the practice of running water through the iron ore after it has been dug from the ground, which has the effect of removing the soil and excess shale waste,

Some areas of early surface ironstone workings for the Penydarren Ironworks, established in Merthyr Tydfil in 1784, have survived on Merthyr Common.

leaving a more concentrated ore to be transported to the iron furnaces. Scouring leaves deep, wide gullies, which are the easiest part of the archaeology to recognise. A significant area of scouring, which incorporates evidence of watercourses, dam and scour, survives just above a housing estate at Winch Fawr (SO 0179 0695), close to the A465 Heads of the Valleys road on the outskirts of Merthyr.

Evidence of early mining is found on Merthyr Common at Ffos y Fran (SO 071 057), a landscape covered in shallow pits and spoil heaps, but also where there are remains of a former squatter settlement, with the outlines of cottages and gardens clearly visible. The land was part of the minerals lease for Penydarren Ironworks, but just next to it are former reservoirs supplying water to the Dowlais Ironworks. This huge (by contemporary standards) ironworks had an insatiable need for water to work the wheels in its forges, which it drew from extensive gathering grounds on the east side of Merthyr. There are several surviving ponds – Sarn Howell Pond (SO 0756 0590), Penydarren Pond (SO 0779 0636), Isaac Morgan Pond (SO 0828 0624), Shepherd's Pond (SO 0929 0645) and Rhaslas Pond (SO 0950 0718) – in a landscape where there are fragmentary remains of old railways, as well as pits and spoil heaps associated with working both ironstone and coal.

The best place to see evidence of ironstone (and coal) extraction is on the hills above Blaenavon, which is now a World Heritage Site in recognition of the importance of this period of Welsh history. (The national and international status of the Merthyr Tydfil iron industry has unfortunately not warranted World Heritage status because so much of its heritage has been lost.) At Penffordd Goch pond (SO 2551 1087), which is on the south-west side of the Blorenge, patches and scours with cliff-like edges can be seen quite close to the road and near the pond car park, as well as evidence of small ponds and the leats that were dug to channel water to them. The pond itself was created out of an old scour to act as a reservoir feeding Garnddyrys Forge, described below, and the Brecknock and Abergavenny Canal (now part of the Monmouthshire & Brecon Canal). On these hills, there are extensive remains of tramways as well as twentieth-century opencast workings, which provide a stark contrast with the earlier workings and, of course, destroyed plenty of archaeological evidence in their making. These are not the prettiest of industrial remains, and the poorly-drained nature of the landscape gives some insight into the environmental damage caused by this kind of surface working.

The Blaenavon iron ore workings are part of an extensive industrial landscape, where coal was also exploited. The main blast furnace site is in Blaenavon town, but the forges where the pig iron was converted to malleable wrought iron occupy an upland site on the west side of the Blorenge, close to the road between Blaenavon and Abergavenny. This is Garnddyrys, built in 1817. Its position on high ground was unusual (and it was later superseded by a new forge in Blaenavon town), but it was well-placed for transport to the canal. It also derived its motive power from waterwheels, making the most of the abundant supply of water from the hills. In addition to Penffordd Goch pond on the summit of the hill, another pond, now dry, is next to the works itself. Although the layout of the works is not really apparent from the earthwork remains, the tramroads and the ponds show how it was connected to the wider landscape.

Penffordd Goch, also known as Keeper's Pond, above Blaenavon (Torfaen), supplied water to Garnddyrys Forge and the Brecknock & Abergavenny Canal. It was created from an old ironstone surface working.

This restored wooden aqueduct was built in 1876 as part of the well-established Dowlais gathering grounds that crossed the new Bargoed Taf branch of the Great Western and Rhymney Railway near Merthyr Tydfil.

The gathering grounds for the Dowlais Ironworks near Merthyr Tydfil, consisted of reservoirs and watercourses that stored and channelled water for the ironworks. The evidence has partially survived in a landscape of ancient and modern mining remains.

This elongated, wide gulley on the hills above Blaenavon (Torfaen) is what
remains of a scour, a typical feature of the iron-mining landscape.

COAL MINING

There are coalfields in both north and south Wales. The South
Wales Coalfield is by far the largest and extends across the old counties of Glamorgan and Monmouthshire to the edge of the Bannau
Brycheiniog National Park. There is an extension of the coalfield further west in west Carmarthenshire, continuing into Pembrokeshire.
The North Wales coalfield is much smaller and, because of its thinner
seams, much less productive. There are coal deposits in Flintshire, but
the largest reserves were in the historical boundary of Denbighshire,
around Wrexham, where there were also iron ore deposits and an iron
industry. Not all of these colliery operations were found in upland
landscapes. For practical reasons, it is the South Wales Coalfield where
evidence of coal mining is likely to be found on the open hills. Here
the coal deposits originated in three distinct geological layers – the
Upper, Middle and Lower Coal Measures. The prosperity of the South
Wales coal industry in the nineteenth and early twentieth century was
based on exploiting the Middle and Lower Coal Measures. The Upper

Coal Measures have comparatively less coal, with thinner seams, but also include Pennant sandstone which was an excellent building material. The Middle and Lower Coal Measures outcrop at the north end of the coalfield, which explains why the first fortunes in the coal industry were made along the heads of the valleys.

A traditional image of a colliery would be much like the restored examples at Big Pit and Rhondda Heritage Park: dominated by the winding gear that reaches for the sky like a church spire, surrounded by engine houses, washing houses and a network of railways. The importance of the transport infrastructure meant that the large collieries were usually to be found on the valley floor – Big Pit is unusual in this respect as it is found in a landscape that would otherwise be described as upland. Large collieries in the twentieth century had large spoil tips that once were a common sight on the valley sides and tops. Large spoil tips are a product of the use of explosives in the mines, which began in the second half of the nineteenth century. When the coal seams were

Large piles of clinker are one of the signs of large-scale ironworking activity, as here at Garnddyrys Forge, on the west side of the Blorenge (Torfaen), part of the Blaenavon Ironworks.

dug entirely by hand, there was much less waste material brought to the surface, for obvious reasons. To transport spoil a safe distance from the pit head, complex inclined planes were sometimes necessary.

It is remarkable how much evidence of the coal industry has disappeared from the landscapes of South Wales. Colliery buildings have been removed from the valley floors, networks of railways taken up. Large hillside spoil tips were never a long-term solution, even without the tragedy of Aberfan where, in 1966, an unstable tip subsided and killed 144 people in the valley below. So much of the upland re-landscaping has involved the removal of tips, although there remain some examples that cause serious concerns for people living close by. Added to the physical removal of infrastructure and waste, we have to take into account that exploitation of coal associated with ironmaking, especially along the heads of the valleys in South Wales, was intensive, producing a complex mining landscape. The problem with this for the archaeologist is that the rapid development of the iron industry in Wales in the latter half of the

A restored incline winding drum built in the mid-nineteenth century to convey coal from early coal levels down to the Sirhowy valley (Tredegar), where Bedwellty Pits were later opened.

Opencast coal mining on Dowlais Top has transformed the ancient mining landscape near Merthyr Tydfil.

eighteenth century took place where the mineral deposits were closest to the surface. Where coal was dug from a series of small pits 200 years ago, today it can be extracted from the surface using heavy machinery; so much of the early coal-mining evidence has suffered the same fate as early iron-ore mining. Large opencast mines destroy evidence of earlier extraction and, once completed, need to be re-landscaped to cover over the scars, otherwise known as archaeological evidence.

There are still various types of colliery-related features to be found on the unenclosed hillsides – here, it is the small, early workings that have left the most trace. The earliest evidence of coal mining has left only earthwork evidence. Shallow seams of coal were worked from the surface by means of bell pits and patches, and where they survive they are often intermixed with ironstone workings. An alternative was to drive a level into a sloping hillside where a coal seam was seen to outcrop. These look very similar to the adits of metal mines but can be interpreted as coal workings with confidence if they are found in an area of coal measures. There are some good surviving examples of coal mining landscapes, especially at Clydach Terrace (SO 183 136), north of Brynmawr and the Heads of the Valleys road, where the land has not been re-landscaped. Eventually, however, the easy seams were worked out and underground workings were needed.

Modern opencast mining near Blaenavon (Torfaen) has erased all evidence of early mining here.

When the market for coal justified capital expenditure in its exploitation, coal was exploited from deeper underground, either by means of vertical shafts, or by drifts, which are tunnels driven into the ground at a steep angle. Coal was raised by various means – by manually operated windlass, water-balance lifts and steam-powered winding engines. Water-balance lifts were only possible in shallow, self-draining pits. They worked on a counterweight principle, whereby a tank of water was set on one side of a fulcrum and a loaded wagon in the pit on the other side, allowing the coal to be raised. This technique needed large quantities of water. This is not usually a problem on the Welsh hills, and is evidenced by the number of small ponds and the drainage ditches that filled them, and a simple superstructure to mount a pulley wheel above the pit (an example of which can be seen at Big Pit). The head of a water-balance pit has survived at Cwmbyrgwm Colliery (SO 2521 0326) near Abersychan. Steam engines were also used for pumping; drainage is, and always was, the bane of deep coal mining. Evidence of underground mining to be seen on the surface includes remains of winding and pumping engine houses, which had adjacent boilers (invariably removed for scrap or re-use) and a boiler chimney. Nearby ponds may have been used as a water source. For safety reasons the shafts were plugged when they were abandoned, but they can be identified sometimes as a small fenced-off enclosure, or even the upper levels of a stone or brick-lined pit.

By the end of the nineteenth century, powerful fans were introduced to ventilate underground workings, ideally placed over a separate shaft known as the upcast shaft. Before that a much cruder and less effective system of ventilation shafts, or air shafts, was used. In these, fires were lit at the base of the shafts, the purpose of which was to create a draught of air underground, thereby drawing out all the bad, combustible air in the underground passages and galleries. The locations of these air shafts are clearly marked on the Ordnance Survey maps of the late-nineteenth and early-twentieth century. Very often there is no longer any evidence of these above ground, though sometimes a short chimney stack, usually square and built of stone, has been built over the air shafts to improve their draught.

One of the shafts, now fenced off, at Cwmbyrgwm Colliery (Torfaen).

Several of the coal mining landscapes of South Wales are worth exploring in detail. Of these, the best preserved and, arguably, the most interesting is at Blaenavon, part of a wider industrial landscape that also encompassed ironstone and limestone extraction. Big Pit is an upland colliery where the substantial surviving evidence is the latest phase of a longer history of coal mining. Most of the surviving buildings at Big Pit belong to the twentieth century, but work began here in the early-nineteenth century to supply coal to the Blaenavon Ironworks, and was stepped up after a new forge was built nearby on the south side of the town. There are numerous features just beyond the bounds of the museum. The earlier workings here were known as Coity Pits (the fan at Big Pit is built over the Coity Pit shaft of 1840) and there are spoil tips, reservoirs (SO 2330 0903 and SO 2364 0872) and the leats that fed it on the hillside above the pit.

Garn yr Erw, on the north-west side of Blaenavon, has an unenclosed landscape of former collieries, centred around the visually conspicuous remains of Hill Pits (SO 2392 1028). The pit was sunk in the

The engine house for a Cornish beam pumping engine was built by the British Ironworks, near Abersychan, in 1845, to drain the company's collieries.

The chimney is the most conspicuous surviving feature of Cwmbyrgwm Colliery near Abersychan (Torfaen). Probably dating from the 1870s it stands over an air shaft.

late 1830s, and by 1893 was linked underground with another colliery, known as Tunnel Pit. Although the shafts were infilled in 1963, one of them, surrounded by a wooden fence, is clearly identifiable. The position of a former winding-engine house is recognisable by the surviving stone chimney stack. But there are earlier features here too. Hill Pits stands on a ridge where there are the remains of several other collieries. Most of them have associated ponds that were used to store water for the water-balance lifts. All of these needed to be filled with rainwater, so there is also a complex system of drains, or leats, to fill them, which criss-cross the landscape. This is also a landscape of small quarries to provide building stone, spoil tips and the remains of former tramways, used before standard gauge railways became the norm for large collieries, although there is an impressive incline, known as Dyne Steel's Incline, which carried coal over the hill to Garnddyrys Forge on a standard-gauge railway. The steam engine that hauled wagons up the slope has gone. There are also enclosures here that belonged to

The setting of Big Pit (Torfaen) against open moorland is a reminder of the impact that large collieries must have made in the upland landscape.

smallholdings, which reminds us that industrial and rural work often went hand-in-hand for much of the nineteenth century, while the former presence of terraced houses is now difficult to pick out. Walk uphill to the north-west and you will encounter a large area of modern opencast working, within which is a maze of tracks and with minimum biodiversity – the modern face of coal extraction.

WATER

Water is one of the chief natural resources of Wales, and ponds and lakes are a regular feature of the landscape. Its use in industry has already been described earlier in this chapter, and covers water for waterwheels, hushing and scouring, to supply steam engines and for use in water-balance lifts. From the nineteenth century, water from the uplands has also been impounded for domestic water supply. The majority of these schemes are small-scale, developed by local water boards to supply mostly rural districts. There are a large number of them across the uplands of Wales. Many were developed from natural lakes, which invariably meant raising the level of the impounded water by building a dam at its lowest point. Eryri has several examples such as Llyn Morwynion, by Ffestiniog Urban District Council and Llyn Cwmystradllyn, built in 1959 to supply the Llŷn Peninsula and the Eifionydd district of Caernarfonshire. Llyn Arenig Fawr has been supplying water to Bala from about 1830, in the early days by means of an over-ground iron pipe. Llyn Cowlyd has supplied the Conwy and Colwyn Bay area since 1891, but its pipe network is underground.

Some of these converted lakes are no longer required as reservoirs. Llyn Anafon in the Carneddau range was dammed in 1931 but is no longer in use. Llyn Llygad Rheidol (SN 7915 8765) near Plynlimon is a natural lake shaped by rocky outcrops on three sides. It is the source of the Rheidol river; but, from 1883, it was also a reservoir supplying water to Aberystwyth. Contemporary Ordnance Survey maps show a pump installed on its north side, from where the water was piped 13 miles west to the town. The lake was later superseded by the more ambitious scheme of Nant y Moch. The 1955 North Wales Hydro-Electric Act was the beginning of an upgrade to the water supply, that required building the reservoir at Nant y Moch, and a smaller reservoir downstream at Dinas, completed in 1964 when the Rheidol Hydro-Electric scheme was officially opened. It is still the largest hydro-electric scheme in Wales.

These small reservoirs are found in upland locations, usually where there is no surrounding settlement. Where the reservoirs were created, there were restrictions on farming the gathering grounds above them. At Llyn Cwmystradllyn, farmsteads immediately above the water line were abandoned when the reservoir was built, not least because the water level was raised by means of a dam.

The best-known and most controversial of reservoir schemes are those that flooded river valleys by erecting a high dam. In the nineteenth and twentieth centuries, opposition to them came from various quarters, encompassing concerns over the future of grazing rights and the loss of common rights in general, as well as the negative impact on natural scenery. These concerns were echoed in the reservoir schemes in upland England, but in Wales they also stirred up nationalist feeling when large tracts of upland were lost to provide water for English cities: chiefly Liverpool in the 1870s with the Vyrnwy scheme and Birmingham in the 1890s with the much larger Elan Valley scheme. *Cofiwch Dreweryn!* – 'remember Tryweryn!' – became a rallying cry for Welsh nationalism after a private members bill sponsored by Liverpool City Council passed through Parliament in 1962, for flooding the Tryweryn Valley, and the village of Capel Celyn along with it, to provide water for Liverpool. By obtaining an Act of Parliament, Liverpool bypassed the need to seek planning permission from local authorities, and in the House of Commons most MPs representing Welsh constituencies voted against it in both readings, while none voted for it. But the Welsh MPs were outnumbered by English votes, leaving Wales with a bitter sense of its own powerlessness. The reservoir – known as Llyn Celyn – has remained controversial, but it was not the first time that large reservoir schemes have kindled nationalist sentiment. When the Birmingham Corporation Water Bill was passing through

One of the shafts at Hill Pits, near Blaenavon (Torfaen), has now been fenced off.

The chimney at Hill Pits above Blaenavon (Torfaen). The pit was sunk in the 1830s and the boiler stack served a steam winding engine.

One of the reservoirs near Hill Pits, Blaenavon (Torfaen). It originally supplied a water balance lift for raising coal from shallow pits, but later probably provided water for the boilers at Hill Pits.

Parliament in 1892, the MP for Swansea District, Henry Vivian, felt that the mountains of Wales were treated as nothing more than waste ground: 'the Members for Birmingham and London regard Wales as a carcass which is to be divided between them according to their own wants and wishes'.

One of the arguments for building large reservoirs, beyond the immediate need to solve the public health crises of Victorian Britain, was their recreational potential, beautifying landscapes and attracting visitors. Apart from Llyn Celyn, which remains a curiously barren place, this has largely come to pass, especially in the Elan Valley which is becoming increasing popular as a leisure destination. These large reservoirs have certainly made a significant impact on the character of the surrounding upland landscapes, perhaps making them seem more remote than they once were.

In the context of the late-nineteenth century, reservoirs were also regarded as heroic achievements that answered the problems of urban public health and sanitation, and were built in response to various Public Health Acts. In Wales, the first town to enjoy the benefits of water supplied from an artificial reservoir was Merthyr Tydfil, which was then the largest town in Wales and had grown rapidly from the late-eighteenth century – unfortunately in a haphazard, unplanned way that had serious consequences for public health. Cholera outbreaks in 1832, 1849 and 1854 were particularly severe in Merthyr. Fortunately, the Merthyr district is well supplied with rainwater and the town stands at the confluence of the Taf Fawr and Taf Fechan rivers; although the need for domestic water had to compete with, and was delayed by, an extremely powerful industrial lobby that also demanded access to water. The first reservoir, known as Pentwyn, was built between 1858 and 1862 on the Taf Fechan (now at the upper end of Ponsticill Reservoir). Its water was stored behind an earthen dam and was piped, untreated, to the town. A second reservoir was built to serve growing demand in the town and its surrounding area further upstream on the Taf Fechan. Known now as Lower Neuadd, it was completed in 1880 (but is now disused).

Llyn Cwmystradllyn (Gwynedd) is a natural lake that was dammed to create a reservoir in 1959. Tal-y-Llyn farm was abandoned at the same time.

The concrete dam at Nant-y-Moch (Ceredigion), source of water for Aberystwyth.

By this time, technology had advanced enough to enable the construction of high dams that flooded large areas of upland valleys. The first of this new generation was Lake Vyrnwy, a ground-breaking engineering achievement in its time. However, the most ambitious was perhaps the Elan Valley schemes built by the Birmingham Corporation in the 1890s. Not all of these large schemes provided water to English cities, but all of them involved displacement of settled communities and farms. Large reservoirs at the southern end of the Bannau Brycheiniog National Park supply much of urbanised South Wales. The Taf Fawr reservoirs beside the A470 at Llwyn-Onn (1926), Cantref (1892) and Beacons (1897) were built to supply Cardiff. On the Taf Fechan, Upper Neuadd (1902) and Pontsticill (1927) were built to supply the Cardiff valleys. Talybont (1939) supplied Newport. Llyn Brianne, in Powys, which opened in 1973 in the upper reaches of the Tywi, serves a wide swathe of South Wales including Neath and Swansea, and as far west as Llanelli.

Like Nant-y-Moch, many of these reservoirs have subsidiary purposes. Llyn Clywedog, a scheme which was also targeted by Welsh nationalist activists, opened in 1967 and regulates the flow of water in the River Severn (providing limited protection for the Severn towns downstream when the river is in flood) for environmental and public-health reasons, as well as ensuring that there is sufficient water for extraction in the Shropshire and Gloucestershire stretches of the river. Likewise Llyn Brianne regulates the flow of Afon Tywi, as well as supplying water to Swansea and Neath. A small hydro-electric scheme was later built there. Llyn Brenig, completed in 1976, regulates the flow of the River Dee, as well as supplying water to Merseyside, supplementing the earlier Llyn Alwen, completed in 1921. The role of Nant y Moch in providing water for hydroelectricity is mentioned above. Llyn Cowlyd and Llyn Conwy also supply water to a hydro-electric scheme at Dolgarrog in the Conwy Valley.

The typical features of large-scale reservoirs are the dams, built of concrete or of substantial masonry faces around a thick core of clay, earth and rubble, and wide enough to incorporate a roadway on the top of the dam. The outlet of water was controlled by means of valve

The high dam at Graig Goch reservoir, the highest of the reservoirs in the Elan Valley (Powys).

towers which, in the case of the Elan Valley and Vyrnwy reservoirs, are striking architectural compositions. Excess water flows over the top of the dam and down a spillway, helping to keep the natural flow of water moving. Processing works are found below the dams themselves. These are water treatment works, where the water was passed through a series of filter beds, although they are not present at every reservoir.

Llyn y Fan Fach in Carmarthenshire (SN 8020 2180) is a glacial cwm in the south-western Black Mountains of the Bannau Brycheiniog National Park, well-known to walkers and wild swimmers. The lake was converted into a reservoir to serve Llanelli Rural District Council during the First World War. Much of the labouring work was done by conscientious objectors who were housed in a work camp on the site (originally intended for Irish navvies), although no significant evidence

The valve tower on the Graig Goch dam (Powys), from where the outflow of water is controlled, is built in 'Birmingham Baroque' style.

The treatment works below Llyn y Fan Fach reservoir (Carmarthenshire).

of the temporary encampment survives now. Evidently, explosives were used in the provision of stone for construction as there is a former magazine at the foot of the hill, near to the car park. The project was completed in 1918 and the reservoir was in service until 1967, since when it has been maintained as a reserve reservoir. The various structures below the reservoir are typical of contemporary water schemes, albeit on a much smaller scale than the major projects already described, and are easy to see on foot as you walk up from the car park to the lake. The dam is built of masonry and concrete across one corner of the natural lake, raising its level slightly. The water flowed down to filter beds: a large, square, open structure where the flow of water was filtered and was controlled by means of a valve house. The watercourses are crossed by contemporary bridges, which gave access to the dam across difficult terrain, while the natural streams have been modified into artificial channels by building stone walls, with provision for stop planks to regulate the flow.

The Elan Valley reservoirs are built on a completely different scale to Llyn y Fan Fach. The Elan river is a tributary of the River Wye and was long considered a viable source of water for Victorian cities. For a time its flow was monitored as a potential source of water for London. In the event it was the Birmingham Corporation that undertook a massive scheme in the uplands between 1893 and 1904, engineered by James Mansergh, including four high masonry dams and an aqueduct to Birmingham 78 miles long, the course of which can be followed over the lowland landscape of Radnorshire. A fifth dam was completed in 1952, which created the Claerwen reservoir. The reservoirs, water treatment works and hydro-electricity generating schemes at the lowest of the reservoirs, Caban Coch, have survived. However, the temporary encampment for the workforce, and the railway constructed to bring materials to the site, have vanished (although the road on the shore of Caban Coch reservoir follows the original line of the Elan Valley railway). A new village was built below the reservoir to provide homes for maintenance workers. The reservoirs now dominate the Elan and Claerwen valleys, but the surrounding mountains are rich in archaeological evidence from prehistory to the nineteenth century.

The Claerwen reservoir (Powys), with a high concrete dam,
was added to the original Elan Valley scheme and opened in 1952.

9

DEFENCE

A NCIENT defensive sites were not built solely for military purposes and we have encountered many of them already. Earlier sites that had a defensive function, like the Iron Age hillforts, also had other functions, mainly as places of habitation. Likewise medieval castles were defensible, but much of their purpose was an expression of status, while their principal use was residential. Roman defensive sites were also places of habitation, which is where a simple classification of sites runs into difficulty. However, Roman sites are described here because they were established by an army, rather than for individuals, and were primarily military in function, and provided accommodation for soldiers only while on duty.

Progress of the Roman army across southern England was swift following the invasion of AD 43. But in the more mountainous districts of Wales, victory was slower and less decisive. A campaign of AD 48 across the River Dee successfully isolated the people of North Wales from the uplands in the north of England. In South Wales, the territory of the Silures, resistance was still fierce and victory was delayed. Anglesey was attacked in AD 61 and, following the campaign led by the Roman general Agricola in AD 78, Wales, if not fully pacified, was under Roman control as a militarised zone. During this period of campaigning the Roman army was active in the uplands and, even if its interest covers a relatively short period, it left a large body of evidence behind. The legionary fortresses of the Roman army occupy lowland, riverside sites, such as Chester by the Dee and Caerleon by the River Usk. But on campaigns in the AD 70s, forts were built as temporary garrisons, some of which became more permanent, and the army built even more temporary marching camps during their summer movements.

Garrisons were also built in lowland areas, such as Forden Gaer and Caersws on the Severn, and Segontium on the Arfon near Caernarfon. But there are exceptions to this rule, notably at Gelligaer (ST 134 971) between the Rhymney and Bargoed Taf rivers, and at Tomen-y-Mur described below. These were campaign forts built in the 70s that were strengthened in the early second century in order to accommodate a garrison of around 500 auxiliary troops. Where they originally had earthwork defences, perhaps topped by a wooden palisade, they were now strengthened in stone. Permanent garrisons attracted civilian settlement, known as a *vicus*, which is one of the ways in which they are distinguished from the marching camps.

Marching camps cover large areas and were used to hold substantial detachments of troops on summer campaigns or manoeuvres, who would retire to more permanent garrisons in the winter. Like forts, they are rectangular in plan and have few features other than the earthen bank and ditch that surrounded them. This makes them difficult to identify on the ground – many of them were discovered only by aerial photography – although the known ones are marked on the Ordnance Survey maps.

Tomen-y-Mur (SH 709 385) is one of the best-preserved archaeological landscapes in Wales. It was founded probably in AD 77–78 during Agricola's campaigns in north-west Wales. The site at this time comprised a large rectangular enclosure bounded by a bank and ditch, probably with a timber palisade. In c.120 the fort was reduced in size but made more permanent by the erection of stone walls on the ramparts. (This phase is dated by the survival of nine inscribed stones that recorded the work, all of which are now dispersed in different locations.) The long-term occupation of Tomen-y-Mur also made it a residential centre and it has some of the features we normally associate with the idea of a settlement. Outside of the ramparts is an array of ancillary structures, many of

The amphitheatre at Tomen y Mur.

types that were usually found outside Roman forts but which have been destroyed by subsequent development in less-remote locations. A small amphitheatre is easily recognisable by the road, despite the fact that a quarry track was later cut across it. Next to it is a level area used as a parade ground. Remains of a bathhouse, *mansio* (wayside guest house), bridge, aqueducts and burial mounds can also be seen on the ground.

Further south-east at Dol-ddinas, 3km from Tomen-y-Mur, are the remains of five practice camps built by the Roman army, which are the best-preserved of 18 practice camps in the vicinity of the fort (SH 734 378). Practice camps are rectangular earthworks, used to train recruits in the construction of temporary camps, and generally occur in clusters. Tomen-y-Mur has the best-preserved group in Wales, in a landscape that has remained relatively undisturbed, although there are also examples on Gelligaer Common close to the Roman fort there.

Despite a number of conflicts in the centuries following Edward I's Conquest of Wales – the revolt of Owain Glyndŵr, the Wars of the Roses and the Civil Wars – the uplands are free of newly-built military

The original extent of Tomen-y-Mur Roman fort (Gwynedd) is easy to discern in this aerial view, as is the smaller, later phase of occupation and the medieval motte built on the site.

structures until the latter part of the nineteenth century. The Cardwell Reforms of the early 1870s (named after the Secretary of State for War) were intended to provide Britain with a modern professional army based on localised battalions. In effect this meant more battalions. The Welch Regiment was created in 1881 to supplement the already established Royal Welsh Fusiliers and the South Wales Borderers. In response to weaknesses identified in the wake of the Boer War (1899–1902), the Territorial Army was established in 1908. All of these new measures required land to be given over for training purposes, some of which was in the uplands (many coastal sites were also used by the army and, subsequently, the Royal Air Force, for training and exercises). Demands on land for training self-evidently became more pressing during the 1914–18 and 1939–45 wars.

Specific features related to training facilities include evidence of rifle ranges, practice trenches and small arms and artillery firing positions. Rifle ranges are not easy to identify, but many of them were marked on the county-series Ordnance Survey maps of the late-nineteenth and early-twentieth centuries. Associated features that may have survived include the mounds of earth that were used as butts in the same manner as archery butts (which can bear a striking resemblance to long barrows or pillow mounds, depending on their size), and observation huts which were sometimes protected from the line of fire by an earthen bank known as a mantlet. Practice trenches were dug in various configurations, including linear, L-shaped and zig-zag trenches, although most of these were subsequently backfilled and are therefore not easy to identify.

The firing range at Bronaber (SH 734 315), near Trawsfynydd, preserves an extensive range of features associated with army firepower and methods employed in the first half of the twentieth century, and is the best preserved upland military landscape of the period in Wales. It was one of the main practice ranges used by the Royal Artillery. Aside from its relatively sparse population, it was chosen for its undulating landscape, allowing targets to be chosen out of the line of sight. The farms were requisitioned and the inhabitants moved out following the designation of the firing range in the Military Manoeuvres Bill of 1900, and it was fully functioning by the outbreak of war in 1914. There are various features here associated with army practices. These include zig-zag trenches dug during the First World War, trenches for mortars and machine-gun posts, telephone junction boxes used as part of the communications network, and well-fortified observation posts from where performance could be assessed. The range closed in 1958, when part of it was given over to forestry. The remainder has been surveyed in detail, revealing numerous sites, many of which seem small, inconsequential and difficult to recognise if the eye is not already alerted to the possibility of seeing them: mainly small earthworks associated with trenches, firing positions or weapons pits.

Rifle targets set up on the hills near Blaenavon (Torfaen) in the 1870s, with an earthen butt behind it.

The bunker behind the rifle butt near Blaenavon, used as an observation hut.

During the Second World War, anti-invasion defences were built in Britain from 1940 until 1942, by which time the invasion of the Soviet Union had allayed fears that Germany would invade Britain. The possibility of a German attack from the west, via the Republic of Ireland, meant that defences were built in Wales. Although they were focussed on the coast, inland defences were designed to impede the progress of an invading army. Known as inland stop lines, several were built along the courses of major rivers, such as the Wye and Towy, but there were also cross-country lines that extended over uplands and were designed to protect important routes, including mountain passes. Self-evidently, features associated with these defences are found close to roads. The Western Command Stop Line 21 was a line between Rhyl, Corwen, Bala, Dolgellau and Machynlleth. Its best-known feature is the line of large stone tank traps (SH 7956 1725) that spans the pass of Bwlch Oerddws between Dolgellau and Dinas Mawddwy, although remnants survive of a similar line of traps on the section by the A487

A firing position on the Bronaber range (Gwynedd).

The blockhouse built on the Bronaber firing range (Gwynedd) was used to gauge the accuracy of artillery fire.

between Dolgellau and Machynlleth. Western Command Stop Line 23 was between Bangor, Capel Curig and Porthmadog. In Eryri it pro-tected the route inland from the sea above Pen-y-Pass, where the roads from Beddgelert and Llanberis meet en route towards Capel Curig and the A5. The junction of the main roads, near Pen-y-Gwryd Hotel, is well defended with pill boxes on both sides of the road (SH 6605 5572 and SH 6611 5598). All these structures are built of rubble stone, blend-ing with the landscape to some extent, giving them some disguise and quite different from the War Office's usual use of concrete.

In South Wales, the Severn Sub-Area Defence Scheme line between Quakers Yard and Storey Arms, just above the Beacons Reservoir and on the A470, also has a series of surviving defensive features at the latter. In a steep-sided, narrow valley, tank traps (SN 9871 1942) offered a first line of defence, followed by a series of pillboxes and infantry support trenches (SN 9880 1980) where the meanders in the river make for difficult terrain, even for tanks.

Wales was used extensively for training by the RAF in the Second World War. Crash sites litter the uplands, a consequence of a number of factors, not just inexperienced crews in wartime, but also the combination of undulating terrain and bad weather. Not all accidents have led to fatalities – in 1940 a Fairey Battle crash-landed close to Carn Bica in the Preseli Mountains, but its crew escaped unscathed. Many crash sites have left no permanent trace. When aircraft hit the ground at speed, debris is scattered over a wide area, and souvenir hunters have been known to carry off surviving parts. But some crash sites have accompanying memorials. In December 1940 an RAF Wellington bomber crashed in the Bannau Brycheiniog National Park near Cefn yr Ystrad (SO 0894 1370). The site, still strewn with metal fragments, has a commemorative cairn and a wooden cross, plus two brass plaques in memory of the crew, all of whom were killed. Two aircraft have crashed on the summit of Arenig Fawr. A US Army Air Forces B-17

Tank traps on the A470 between Dolgellau and Dinas Mawddwy (Gwynedd) are part of the Western Command Stop Line 23.

Flying Fortress crashed there in 1943 and there is a plaque on the site of a denuded cairn to commemorate the crew, all of whom perished (SH 8270 3695). Just to the south is a site, protected under the Protection of Military Remains Act 1986, where an RAF Folland Gnat crashed in 1964, after its crew had safely ejected on a training flight.

Post-Second World War, the most extensive area in Wales used for military training is at Sennybridge, after plans to use the Preseli Hills were successfully fought off. The Training Area occupies a large tract of Mynydd Epynt and has been in use since it was first identified as a suitable area for training in 1940. During the Second World War it was used by British and other Allied troops. Access to these upland areas is restricted according to military activity, and the land was not designated as Access land in 2000, meaning that exploration of the area is confined to the public rights of way. In these areas, archaeological features are similar to those of the early twentieth century – mainly

This Second World War pillbox, faced in local stone rather than the normal concrete, is near Pen y Gwrd Hotel (Gwynedd), and guards the pass between Beddgelert and Capel Curig.

Tank traps near Storey Arms in Bannau Brycheiniog National Park straddle the A470, and are part of a complex of features defending the narrow valley near the pass over the mountain.

earthworks associated with trenches (of various configurations), firing positions and gun emplacements (large field guns require a flat surface to fire from). There is a Live Firing Range and Impact Area where access is restricted and where there has been some damage to archaeological remains. But there is also a Dry Training Area where there has been far less disturbance than in many upland areas in modern times, which has had the happy consequence that its archaeology is especially well-preserved.

10

LEISURE AND PLEASURE

EVER since the Welsh mountains became a place for visitors, the uplands have had an archaeology of the leisure industry. Most activities have left little evidence behind. Wild campers should leave no trace; hikers are supposed to leave only footprints – the exception being the placing of stones in piles on summits, creating small cairns.

Fishing was once part of a commoner's rights, but by the nineteenth century, these rights were frequently reinterpreted as 'illegal' poaching. Fishing is a practice or pastime that is rarely mentioned in the literature and leaves little archaeological trace. In 1860 the visiting Salopian John Randall learned of men in Llanidloes who earned a sort of living by fishing in the upper reaches of the Severn. In 1920, in his *Book of the Severn*, A.G. Bradley complained that a Welshman 'really believes in his heart that he has a traditional and inalienable right to his share of the fish', but that men who catch fish by 'nefarious means' were 'public enemies'. Fishermen have continued to seek the peace and quiet of the lakeshore or the riverbank, leaving little behind except for the occasional stone-built shelter wall to protect them from inclement weather. Boating once took place on many of Wales' upland lakes, either for fishing or just pleasure, sometimes leaving easily identifiable shoreline boathouses.

Landowners have had no qualms about building where it suits, the most obvious (and arguably egregious) example being the mountain railway and summit café on Yr Wyddfa, now in its umpteenth iteration.

One of the small shelters by Llyn y Manod (Gwynedd) that were probably built by fishermen to protect against inclement weather.

After Yr Wyddfa, the peaks that attracted the most travellers in the past were Cadair Idris and Plynlimon. Generations of huts, hotels and cafés on the summit of Yr Wyddfa have already been described, but Cadair Idris also has a summit building. In the early nineteenth century Richard Pugh established himself as a tour guide in Dolgellau, taking visitors to local waterfalls and to the summit of Cadair Idris. On the latter, as he explained in a poster printed in 1833:

> he is happy to inform those families who wish to visit Cader Idris [sic] for the future, that (although in indigent circumstances) he has been able to furnish a small cottage (eight yards long, 4 yards wide and 2 yards and 6 inches high) on the summit of Cader Idris! which will enable a large party to dine comfortably in, without being exposed to the inclemency of the weather.

It was ideal for visitors who wanted to watch the sun rise from the summit but who preferred not to climb the hill at night. By the time Francis Kilvert was taken there by Pugh's son in 1871, it was draughty, doorless and windowless. The building on the summit today, which is known as Penygadair (SH 7111 1306), is described as a shelter, but appears to be a partial restoration of Pugh's earlier building.

The only other outdoor pursuit to have made a permanent impact on the landscape is grouse shooting. Red grouse is a species unique to the British Isles and was known as the 'king of gamebirds'. It had been hunted since the seventeenth century – Richard Warner encountered a party of grouse-shooters at the Lion Inn in Rhayader in 1797 – but the heyday of the grouse shoot in Wales was from the late-nineteenth until the mid-twentieth century. The advent of the railways made upland regions of Wales far more accessible than they had ever been, while the invention of the breech-loading shotgun allowed for rapid reloading – essential for making the most of the continuous stream of target birds and for amateur shooters to bag a reasonable number of kills. The shooting season ran from 12 August to 10 December, and quickly became a fashionable sport for the wealthy. In 1886 *The South Wales*

A shooting stand on the hills above Bala (Gwynedd).

Daily News would report on a large number of grouse shoots to mark the start of the shooting season, including on the Wynnstay Estate and Ruthin Castle Estate in North Wales; as well as those funded by comparatively new money – the Blaenavon Iron and Steel Company had a party out shooting on the Blorenge above Abergavenny. 'Driven grouse shoots' used teams of beaters to drive the grouse to fly up over lines of shooters (or 'Guns'). The shooters and their loaders were concealed behind grouse butts and shooting stands, and in that way are similar to the dug positions of soldiers found in the former ranges. Short drystone walls or, more often, a small pit and a wall, are the most common form of this, but they are not found in isolation. Grouse butts are usually laid out in long lines across the landscape and date from the nineteenth or twentieth century. These structures could be further concealed by laying turves over the top of them – although these, of course, have not survived.

The commercialisation of grouse shooting in the late-nineteenth century allowed landowners to let out their grouse moors to wealthy men who wanted to participate in this trophy sport. To accommodate these paying Guns, there was a shooting lodge, often referred to as a shooting

Remains of a grouse butt on the hills above Bala (Gwynedd).

box. Many of these have been reduced to ground level and are not easily identifiable as shooting boxes, although as relatively modern buildings you would expect to find evidence of a fireplace. Some are marked on the county-series and modern Ordnance Survey maps. The best clue is always the proximity of shooting butts, which helps to identify the ruinous Liberty Hall (SJ 0890 4098) on the hills above Cynwyd, Denbighshire, as a former shooting lodge. This building was in existence in the early-nineteenth century and is one of several shooting boxes that were adapted from older

This monument on the open hill above Varteg and Cwmavon (Torfaen), was set up by Lord Kennard after his dog was accidentally shot on a grouse shoot on August 12 in 1864.

This corrugated-iron building is a former shooting hut in the Berwyn Mountains (Denbighshire).

The ruins of Gwylfa Hiraethog (Denbighshire).

disused dwellings. Another good example is at Hafod y Brenin (SH 6766 2483), north of Dolgellau, where an old stone dwelling has been subsumed within a twentieth-century lodge, with veranda, of weather-boarded walls and corrugated-iron roof. Gwylfa Hiraethog (the watch tower of Hiraethog) is the most ambitious of shooting lodges in Wales, a Jacobethan mansion improbably sited on a rise in bare moorland, designed by Edwin Cooper for Viscount Devonport, Chairman of the Port of London Authority (SH 9472 5906). The building replaced earlier, more modest affairs and boasted 11 principal bedrooms as well as servants' quarters. In 1925 it was put up for sale and has been uninhabited since the 1960s, during which time it has gradually crumbled into a ruin.

Further reading

Bennett, John and Vernon, Robert, *Mines of the Gwydyr Forest*. The authors, 2023

Bick, David, *The Old Copper Mines of Snowdonia*. Pound House, 1985

—, *The Old Metal Mines of Mid Wales*. Pound House, 1993

Brown, David Lewis, *The Elan Valley Clearance*. Logaston Press, 2019

Browne, David and Hughes, Stephen (eds), *The Archaeology of the Welsh Uplands*. RCAHM Wales, 2003

Crew, Peter, and Musson, Chris, *Snowdonia from the Air: Patterns in the landscape*. Snowdonia National Park Authority, 1996

Davies, Dewi, *Welsh Place Names and their Meanings*. Y Lolfa, 2016

Davies, John, *A History of Wales*. Penguin, 2007

Davis, Paul R., *Forgotten Castles of Wales and the Marches*. Logaston Press, 2022

—, *Wales from the Air: history in the hills*. Logaston Press, 2024

Driver, Toby, *The Hillforts of Cardigan Bay: discovering the Iron Age communities of Ceredigion*. Logaston Press, 2021

—, *The Hillforts of Iron Age Wales*. Logaston Press, 2023

Gwyn, David, *Welsh Slate: archaeology and history of an industry*. RCAHM Wales, 2015

Hopewell, David, *Roman Roads in North-West Wales*. Gwynedd Archaeological Trust, 2013

Hughes, Harold and North, Herbert L., *The Old Cottages of Snowdonia*. Snowdonia National Park Society, 1979

Hughes, Herbert, *An Uprooted Community: A history of Epynt*. Y Lolfa, 2023.

Hughes, Stephen, *The Brecon Fforest Tramroads: the archaeology of an early railway system*. RCAHM Wales, 1990

Johnson, Andy and Karen, *Walking the Old Ways of East Breconshire and the Black Mountains*. Logaston Press, 2022

—, *Walking the Old Ways of Radnorshire*. Logaston Press, 2023

Knight, Jeremy, *Blaenavon: from Iron Town to World Heritage Site*. Logaston Press, 2016

Leighton, D.K., *The Western Bannau Brycheiniog: The archaeology of Mynydd Ddu and Fforest Fawr*. RCAHM Wales, 2012

Lock, Gary, *Moel-y-Gaer (Bodfari): A small hillfort in Denbighshire, North Wales.* Archaeopress Archaeology 2022

Lynch, Frances, *Excavations in the Brenig Valley: A Mesolithic and Bronze Age Landscape in North Wales.* Cambrian Archaeological Association, Monograph No 5, 1993

Marshall, Des, *The Mountain Lakes of Snowdonia.* Llygad Gwalch Cyf, 2020

Moore-Colyer, Richard, *Roads and Trackways of Wales.* Landmark Publishing, 2002

Napier, Jean, *Rhinogydd: Ancient Routes and Old Roads.* Llygad Gwalch Cyf, 2017

Nash, George, *Neolithic Tombs of Wales.* Logaston Press, 2024

Olding, Frank, *The Archaeology of Upland Gwent.* RCHAM Wales, 2016

Silvester, Robert J., *Mynydd Hiraethog: The Denbigh Moors.* RCAHM Wales, 2011

Timberlake, Simon, *Excavations on Copa Hill, Cwmyswyth: An Early Bronze Age Copper Mine in the Uplands of Central Wales.* British Archaeological Reports (British Series 348), 2003

Williams, David, *The Welsh Cistercians.* Gracewing, 2001

INDEX